Preface

The Academic Phrasebank is a general resource for academic writers. It aims to provide the phraseological 'nuts and bolts' of academic writing organised according to the main sections of a research paper or dissertation. Other phrases are listed under the more general communicative functions of academic writing.

The resource was designed primarily for academic and scientific writers who are non-native speakers of English. However, native writers may still find much of the material helpful. In fact, recent data suggest that the majority of users are native speakers of English.

The phrases, and the headings under which they are listed, can be used simply to assist you in thinking about the content and organisation of your own writing, or the phrases can be incorporated into your writing where this is appropriate. In most cases, a certain amount of creativity and adaptation will be necessary when a phrase is used.

The Academic Phrasebank is not discipline specific. Nevertheless, it should be particularly useful for writers who need to report their empirical studies. The phrases are content neutral and generic in nature; in using them, therefore, you are not stealing other people's ideas and this does not constitute plagiarism.

Most of the phrases in this compendium have been organised according to the main sections of a research report. However, it is an over-simplification to associate the phrases only with the section in which they have been placed here. In reality, for example, many of phrases used for referring to other studies may be found throughout a research report.

In the current paperback version, additional material, which is not phraseological, has been included at the end of the document. These additional sections should be helpful to you as a writer.

Dr John Morley, 2023

Academic Phrasebank
Paperback version

5th Edition

The enhanced version of Academic Phrasebank is only available from the website: http://www.phrasebankresearch.net as a PDF file, or from Amazon as a paperback or as a Kindle download.

Contents

About *Academic Phrasebank*

Theoretical Influences

The *Academic Phrasebank* largely draws on an approach to analysing academic texts originally pioneered by John Swales in the 1980s. Utilising a genre analysis approach to identify rhetorical patterns in the introductions to research articles, Swales defined a 'move' as a section of text that serves a specific communicative function (Swales, 1981,1990). This unit of rhetorical analysis is used as one of the main organising sub-categories of the *Academic Phrasebank*. Swales not only identified commonly used moves in article introductions, but he was interested in showing the kind of language which was used to achieve the communicative purpose of each move. Much of this language was phraseological in nature.

The resource also draws upon psycholinguistic insights into how language is learnt and produced. It is now accepted that much of the language we use is phraseological; that it is acquired, stored and retrieved as pre-formulated constructions (Bolinger, 1976; Pawley and Syder, 1983). These insights began to be supported empirically in the 1990s as computer technology permitted the identification of recurrent phraseological patterns in very large corpora of spoken and written English using specialised software (e.g. Sinclair, 1991). The *Phrasebank* recognises that there is an important phraseological dimension to academic language and attempts to make examples of this explicit.

Sources of the phrases

The vast majority of phrases in this resource have been taken from authentic academic sources. The original corpus from which the phrases were 'harvested' consisted of 100 postgraduate dissertations completed at the University of Manchester. However, phrases from academic articles drawn from a broad spectrum of disciplines have also been, and continue to be, incorporated. In most cases, the phrases have been simplified and where necessary they have been 'sifted' from their particularised academic content. Where content words have been included for exemplificatory purposes, these are substitutions of the original words. In selecting a phrase for inclusion into the *Academic Phrasebank*, the following questions are asked:

- does it serve a useful communicative purpose in academic text?
- does it contain collocational and/or formulaic elements?
- are the content words (nouns, verbs, adjectives) generic in nature?
- does the combination 'sound natural' to a native speaker or writer of English?

When is it acceptable to reuse phrases in academic writing?

In a recent study (Davis and Morley, 2015), 45 academics from two British universities were surveyed to determine whether reusing phrases was a legitimate activity for academic writers, and if so, what kind of phrases could be reused. From the survey and later from in-depth interviews, the following characteristics for acceptability emerged. A reused phrase:

- should not have a unique or original construction;
- should not express a clear point of view of another writer;
- depending on the phrase, may be up to nine words in length; beyond this 'acceptability' declines;
- may contain up to four generic content words (nouns, verbs or adjectives which are not bound to a specific topic).

Some of the entries in the *Academic Phrasebank*, contain specific content words which have been included for illustrative purposes. These words should be substituted when the phrases are used. In the phrases below, for example, the content words in bold should be substituted:

- X is a major **public health** problem, and the cause of ...
- In the **new global economy**, X has become a central issue for ...

The many thousands of disciplinary-specific phrases which can be found in academic communication comprise a separate category of phrases. These tend to be shorter than the generic phrases listed in *Academic Phrasebank*, and typically consist of noun phrases or combinations of these. Acceptability for reusing these is determined by the extent to which they are commonly used and understood by members of a particular academic community.

Development of the website content is ongoing. In addition, research is currently being carried out on the ways in which experienced and less-experienced writers make use of the *Academic Phrasebank*. Another project is seeking to find out more about ways in which teachers of English for academic purposes make use of this resource.

References and related reading

- Bolinger, D. (1976) 'Meaning and memory'. *Forum Linguisticum*, 1, pp. 1–14. doi:10.1515/9783110815733.95
- Cowie, A. (1992) 'Multiword lexical units and communicative language teaching' in *Vocabulary and applied linguistics*, Arnaud, P. and Béjoint, H. (eds). London: MacMillan.
- Davis, M., and Morley, J. (2015) 'Phrasal intertextuality: The responses of academics from different disciplines to students' re-use of phrases'. *Journal Second Language Writing* 28 (2), pp. 20-35. doi/10.1016/j.jslw.2015.02.004
- Davis, M. and Morley, J. (2018) in. 'Writing with sources: how much can be copied?' in *Student Plagiarism in Higher Education*, edited by Diane Pecorari and Philip Shaw. Oxford: Routledge. doi/10.4324/9781315166148
- Davis, M. and Morley, J. (2018) "Facilitating learning about academic phraseology: teaching activities for student writers", *Journal of Learning Development in Higher Education*. Special Edition, pp 1- 17. doi: 10.47408/jldhe.v0i0.468
- Davis, M. and Morley, John (2022) 'It can facilitate so much!' Student writers' practice of self-efficacy to develop their use of formulaic phrases' *Journal of Learning Development in Higher Education* 24. doi: 10.47408/jldhe.vi24.856
- Hopkins, A. and Dudley-Evans, A. (1988). 'A genre-based investigations of the discussions sections in articles and dissertation'. *English for Specific Purposes*, 7(2), pp.113-122. doi:10.1016/0889-4906(88)90029-4
- Pawley, A., and Syder, F.H. (1983). 'Two puzzles for linguistic theory: nativelike selection and nativelike fluency'. In: Richards, J.C. and Schmidt, R.W. (Eds.), *Language and communication,* pp. 191-226. Longman: New York.
- Sinclair, J. (1991) *Corpus, concordance, collocation*. Oxford: Oxford University Press.
- Swales, J. (1981). *Aspects of article introductions* (Aston ESP Research Report No. 1). Birmingham: Language Studies Unit: University of Aston.
- Swales, J. (1990). *Genre analysis: English in academic and research settings.* Cambridge: Cambridge University Press.
- Wood, D. (2015) *The fundamentals of formulaic language*. London: Bloomsbury.
- Wray, A., and Perkins, M. (2000). 'The functions of formulaic language: an integrated model'. *Language and Communication,* 20, pp.1-28. doi:10.1016/S0271-5309(99)00015-4

Major Sections

Introducing Work

There are many ways to introduce an academic essay or short paper. Most academic writers, however, appear to do one or more of the following in their introductions:

- establish the context, background and/or importance of the topic
- indicate an issue, problem, or controversy in the field of study
- define the topic or key terms
- state the purpose of the essay or piece of writing
- provide an overview of the coverage and/or structure of the writing

Slightly less complex introductions may simply inform the reader: what the topic is, why it is important, and how the writing is organised. In very short assignments, it is not uncommon for a writer to commence simply by stating the purpose of their writing and by indicating how it is organised.

Introductions to research dissertations and theses tend to be relatively short compared to the other sections of the text but quite complex in terms of their functional elements. Some of the more common elements include:

- establishing the context, background and/or importance of the topic
- giving a brief review of the relevant academic literature
- identifying a problem, controversy or a knowledge gap in the field of study
- stating the aim(s) of the research and the research questions or hypotheses
- providing a synopsis of the research design and method(s)
- explaining the significance or value of the study
- defining certain key terms
- providing an overview of the dissertation or report structure

Examples of phrases which are commonly employed to realise these and other functions are listed under the headings on the following pages of this section. Note that there may be a certain amount of overlap between some of the categories under which the phrases are listed. Also, the order in which the different categories of phrases are shown reflects a typical order but this is far from fixed or rigid, and not all the elements are present in all introductions.

A number of analysts have identified common patterns in the introductions of research articles. One of the best known is the CARS model (create a research space) first described by John Swales (1990)[1]. This model, which utilises an ecological metaphor, has, in its simplest form, three elements or moves:

- Establishing the territory (establishing importance of the topic, reviewing previous work)
- Identifying a niche (indicating a gap in knowledge)
- Occupying the niche (listing purpose of new research, listing questions, stating value, indicating structure of writing)

---

[1] Swales, J. (1990) *Genre Analysis*. Cambridge: Cambridge University Press.

Establishing the importance of the topic for the discipline
A key aspect of X is ...
X is of interest because ...
X is a classic problem in ...
X is a central concept in ...
A primary concern of X is ...
X is a dominant feature of ...
X is a fundamental property of ...
Xs are the most widely investigated ...
Studies on X represent a growing field.
X is an increasingly important area in...
The concepts of X and Y are central to ...
X is at the heart of our understanding of ...
X is attracting considerable critical attention.
Central to the theory of X is the Y hypothesis.
X has been shown to occur in many different ...
Investigating X is a continuing concern within ...
X is a major area of interest within the field of ...
X has been studied by many researchers using ...
X has been the subject of many classic studies in ...
X has been instrumental in our understanding of ...
The theory of X provides a useful account of how ...
X has been an important concept in the study of the ...
Central to the entire discipline of X is the concept of ...
One of the most significant current discussions in X is ...
X has been the subject of much systematic investigation.
The issue of X has received considerable critical attention.
Understanding the complexity of X is vitally important if ...
X has long been a question of great interest in a wide range of fields.
The role of X in Y has received increased attention across a number of disciplines in recent years.

Establishing the importance of the topic for the discipline: time frame given
X was one of the most popular Ys during ...
Recent years have seen renewed interest in ...
Traditionally, Xs have subscribed to the belief that ...
Recent trends in X have led to a proliferation of studies that ...
Recent years have witnessed a growing academic interest in ...
The nature of X has been the subject of several recent papers.
Over the past century, there has been a dramatic increase in ...
X proved an important literary genre in the early Y community.
X has received considerable scholarly attention in recent years ...
In recent years, researchers have shown an increased interest in ...
Recently, considerable literature has grown up around the theme of ...
Recent developments in the field of X have led to a renewed interest in ...
The past thirty years have seen increasingly rapid advances in the field of ...
In the last few decades, there has been a surge of interest in the effects of ...
For more than a century, scientists have been interested in the existence of ...
The most significant recent developments in this direction have been those of ...
The discovery of X in 2016 has triggered a huge amount of innovative scientific inquiry.
During the last decade, the link between X and Y has been at the centre of much attention.

Recently, More recently, In recent years,	there has been	growing interest in ... renewed interest in ... a surge of interest in ... increasing interest in ... extensive research on ... increased emphasis on ... growing recognition of the vital links between ... a growing number of publications focusing on ... a greater focus placed upon X within the Y literature. world-wide recognition of the problems associated with ...

X	has been	studied widely studied extensively an object of research studied using light-microscopy attracting considerable interest	since	the 1960s. it was discovered in 1998. the early years of this century.

Establishing the importance of the topic for the world or society

X is widespread in ...
X is fundamental to ...
X is the primary means of ...
X is a major contributor to ...
X is an important aspect of ...
X is frequently prescribed for ...
The importance of X is indisputable.
X is one of the key components of Y.
Xs are among the most widely used ...
X is fast becoming a key instrument in ...
X is the most widely distributed species of ...
Xs have emerged as powerful platforms for ...
Xs are one of the most widely used groups of ...
Xs are essential for a wide range of technologies.
Xs are the most potent anti-inflammatory agents known.
There is evidence that X plays a crucial role in regulating ...
In the history of X, Y has been thought of as a key factor in ...
X is a common condition which has considerable impact on ...
In the new global economy, X has become a central issue for ...
Determining the impacts of X on Y is important for the future of ...
Evidence suggests that X is among the most important factors for ...
X is important for a wide range of scientific and industrial processes.
X is an important component in the X system, and plays a key role in ...
There is a growing body of literature that recognises the importance of ...
Xs were the most serious and widespread popular disturbances to occur in ...

X	plays a(n) can play a(n) may play a(n)	key vital major crucial pivotal central essential important significant fundamental	role in	ensuring ... reducing ... fostering ... combating ... preventing ... determining ... protecting against ... addressing the issue of ... the repair of ... the life cycle of ... the treatment of ... the regulation of ... the transmission of ... the maintenance of ... the development of ... the pathogenesis of ...

X	is a key	part of ... issue in ... driver of ... factor in ... aspect of ... feature of ... element of ... strategy for ... indicator of ... ingredient in ... component of ... mechanism for ... determinant of ... characteristic of ...

Establishing the importance of the topic for the world or society: time frame given

X has been an established practice since ...
One of the most important events of the 1970s was ...
Recent developments in X have heightened the need for ...
The last two decades have seen a growing trend towards ...
Recent trends in X have led to a proliferation of studies that ...
Over the past century, there has been a dramatic increase in ...
The past decade has seen the rapid development of X in many ...
X has experienced unprecedented growth over the past 100 years.

Establishing the importance of the topic as a problem to be addressed

X is a key issue in ...
X is a leading cause of ...
X is a major problem in ...
Of particular concern is ...
One of the main obstacles ...
One of the greatest challenges ...
X is the leading cause of death in ...
A key issue is the safe disposal of ...
The main disadvantage of X is that ...
X is associated with increased risk of ...
X impacts negatively upon a range of ...
X is a common disorder characterised by ...
It is now well established that X can impair ...
X has led to the decline in the population of ...
X is a growing public health concern worldwide.
The main challenge faced by many researchers is the ...
X is one of the most frequently stated problems with ...
Lack of X has existed as a health problem for many years.
X is a major environmental problem, and the main cause of ...
Xs are one of the most rapidly declining groups of insects in ...
Exposure to X has been shown to be related to adverse effects in ...
There is increasing concern that some Xs are being disadvantaged ...
There is an urgent need to address the safety problems caused by ...
The prevalence of X is increasing at an alarming rate in all age groups.
Questions have been raised about the safety of the prolonged use of ...
Despite its safety and efficacy, X suffers from several major drawbacks:
Along with this growth in X, however, there is increasing concern over ...
X is increasingly recognised as a serious, worldwide public health concern.
Despite its long clinical success, X is associated with a number of problems.
X and its consequences are an important, but understudied, cause for concern.

(However,)	X may cause ... X is limited by ... X suffers from ... X is too expensive to be used for ... X has accentuated the problem of ... the performance of X is limited by ... X could be a contributing factor to ... the synthesis of X remains a major challenge. X can be extremely harmful to human beings. research has consistently shown that X lacks ... the determination of X is technically challenging. a major problem with this kind of application is ... current methods of X have proven to be unreliable. these rapid changes are having a serious effect on ... X can be adversely affected under certain conditions. accounting for these varying experiences is problematic . observations have indicated a serious decline in the population of ...

Referring to previous work to establish what is already known

Recent evidence suggests that ...
Extensive research has shown that ...
Research in this area has shown that ...
Studies of X show the importance of ...
It has previously been observed that ...
Several attempts have been made to ...
Data from several studies suggest that ...
Previous research has established that ...
Recent work by historians has established that ...
Previous research comparing X and Y has found ...
The existing body of research on X suggests that ...
There is a growing body of literature that recognises ...
Several theories on the origin of X have been proposed.
Existing research recognises the critical role played by ...
It is now well established from a variety of studies, that ...
A growing body of published work provides evidence of ...
Recently investigators have examined the effects of X on Y.
Surveys such as that conducted by Smith (1988) have shown that ...
Evidence from a number of experimental studies has established that ...
Factors found to be influencing X have been explored in several studies.
A number of cross-sectional studies suggest an association between X and Y...
Studies over the past two decades have provided important information on ...
A considerable amount of literature has been published on X. These studies ...
In the past two decades, a number of researchers have sought to determine ...
In previous studies of X, different variables have been found to be related to ...
The first serious discussions and analyses of X emerged during the 1970s with ...
There have been a number of longitudinal studies involving X that have reported ...
Xs were reported in the first studies of Y (e.g., Smith, 1977; Smith and Jones, 1977).
What we know about X is largely based upon empirical studies that investigate how ...
Smith (1984: 217) shows how, in the past, research into X was mainly concerned with ...
Results from earlier studies demonstrate a strong and consistent association between ...
There are a large number of published studies (e.g., Smith, 2001; Jones, 2005) that describe ...

It has been	noted that ... found that ... shown that ... argued that ... reported that ... assumed that ... observed that ... proposed that ... estimated that ... suggested that ... established that ... demonstrated that .... conclusively shown that ...

Recent Previous	studies have research has	found ... linked ... reported ... shown that ... documented ... demonstrated ... established that ...

Several A number of	studies researchers	have	found ... reported ... identified .... shown that ... attempted to ... demonstrated that ... investigated whether ... found an association between ... confirmed the effectiveness of ... explored risk factors associated with ... revealed a correlation between X and Y. highlighted factors that are associated with ...

What	we know about X is known about X	comes from is (largely) based on is (largely) derived from	accounts by ... observations of ... laboratory studies. outdated studies ... historical data from ... epidemiological studies. brief biographical details. cross-sectional studies of ... studies of people living in ... case studies undertaken in ... contemporary textual sources. small-scale experiments with ... research using laboratory animals. research undertaken in major cities. a few primary sources from the time. studies conducted in populations of X. observations using various animal models.

Identifying a controversy within the field of study

A much-debated question is whether ...
Debate has long prevailed as to whether ...
The precise effect of X is a much-debated topic.
One major issue in early X research concerned ...
To date there has been little agreement on what ...
The issue has grown in importance in light of recent ...
One of the most significant current discussions in X is ...
There has been disagreement on the criteria for defining X.
One observer has already drawn attention to the paradox in ...
Questions have been raised about the use of animal subjects in ...
In the literature on X, the importance of Y has been hotly debated ...
In many Xs, a debate is taking place between Ys and Zs concerning ...
Debate continues about the best strategies for the management of ...
This concept has recently been challenged by X studies demonstrating ...
There has been much disagreement between historians on the subject of ...
The debate about X has gained fresh prominence with many arguing that ...
Scholars have long debated the impact of X on the creation and diffusion of ...
More recently, literature has emerged that offers contradictory findings about ...
The relationship between X and Y has attracted conflicting interpretations from ...
One major theoretical issue that has dominated the field for many years concerns ...
The controversy about scientific evidence for X has raged unabated for over a century.
The issue of X has been a controversial and much disputed subject within the field of ...
Several divergent accounts of X have been proposed, creating numerous controversies.
The causes of X have been the subject of intense debate within the scientific community.
In the literature on X, the relative importance of Y has been subject to considerable discussion.

So far To date	there has been	no little	agreement	on about	why ... what ... which ... how to ... whether ... how much ... the role of ... the origin of ... the nature of ... the definition of ... what constitutes ... the characteristics of ... the precise nature of ... how best to measure ... how to conduct research on ... the important question of why ...

Noting the lack of or paucity of previous research

No previous study has investigated X.
The use of X has not been investigated.
There is little published information on ...
The role of X remains largely unexamined.
There is very little published research on ...
There has been no detailed investigation of ...
There has been little quantitative analysis of ...
Data about the efficacy and safety of X are limited.
Up to now, far too little attention has been paid to ...
A search of the literature revealed few studies which ...
The impact of X on Y is understudied, particularly for ...
So far, however, there has been little discussion about ...
In addition, no research has been found that surveyed ...
Surprisingly, the effects of X have not been closely examined.
Surprisingly, X is seldom studied, and it is unclear to what extent ...
In contrast to X, there is much less information about effects of ...
X has hitherto received scant attention by scholars of the Y period.
A systematic understanding of how X contributes to Y is still lacking.
While X is a growing field (Smith, 2015), publications on Y remain few.
Relatively little research has been carried out on X, and even less on Y.
Despite the importance of X, there remains a paucity of evidence on ...
There have been no controlled studies which compare differences in ...
The issue of X has attracted very little attention from the scholarly community.
To date, the problem of X has received scant attention in the research literature.
To date, no large-scale studies have been performed to investigate the prevalence of ....
Although studies have recognised X, research has yet to systematically investigate the effect of ...

To date, Surprisingly,	X	has (still) not (yet) been	closely formally empirically extensively scientifically systematically comprehensively	studied. examined. investigated.

<table>
<tr><td rowspan="3">There is a</td><td rowspan="3">current
relative
general
notable
surprising</td><td rowspan="3">lack
paucity</td><td>of studies
of well-controlled studies</td><td>investigating ...
describing how ...
that seek to identify ...</td></tr>
<tr><td>of empirical research
of high-quality research</td><td>in the field of ...
focusing specifically on ...
on the current prevalence of ...</td></tr>
<tr><td>of scientific literature
of evidence-based literature</td><td>specifically relating to ...
on the experiences of ...
describing the impact of ...</td></tr>
</table>

<table>
<tr><td>No previous study has
(Very) few studies have
Few (published) studies have</td><td>explored ...
focused on ...
investigated ...
controlled for ...
examined how ...
compared trends in ...
attempted to define ...
examined the role of ...
measured X in humans.
analysed the impact of ...
quantified the levels of ...
systematically investigated ...
assessed the implications of ...
evaluated the effects of X on ...
examined the consequences of ...
provided quantitative evidence of ...
systematically evaluated the use of ...
attempted to quantify the impact of ...
adequately tested the effectiveness of ...
addressed the long term psychological effects of ...
been large enough to provide reliable estimates of ...
been conducted to determine the possible effects of ...</td></tr>
</table>

<table>
<tr><td rowspan="3">So far,
To date,
Up to now,</td><td>there</td><td>has been no systematic analysis of ...
have been no attempts to examine ...
has been very little research directly investigating X.
have been very few empirically published accounts of X.</td></tr>
<tr><td>(very) little</td><td>research has been carried out on ...
has been published on the subject of ...
attention has been paid to the role of ...
research has addressed the question of ...</td></tr>
<tr><td>(very) few</td><td>studies have assessed the role of ...
studies have examined the association between ...
studies have investigated x in any systematic way ...
randomised clinical trials have specifically investigated X in ...</td></tr>
</table>

Relatively Surprisingly Remarkably Comparatively	few	studies have	analysed ... assessed ... examined ... measured ... investigated ...
	little	research has	

While Whilst Although	some research has been carried out on X,	no single study exists which ... no studies have been found which ... this area has yet to receive attention. no controlled studies have been reported. there is very little scientific understanding of ... only two studies have attempted to investigate ... there have been few empirical investigations into ... the mechanism by which ... has not been established. no studies of the effects of X on Y have been published. little if any empirical work has been done to investigate ...
	several studies have shown that ...,	

Highlighting inadequacies or weaknesses of previous studies (also refer to *Being Critical*)
Previous studies of X have not dealt with ...
Researchers have not treated X in much detail.
Such expositions are unsatisfactory because they ...
Such approaches, however, have failed to address ...
Most studies in the field of X have only focused on ...
Previous published studies are limited to local surveys.
Half of the studies evaluated failed to specify whether ...
The research to date has tended to focus on X rather than Y.
Previously published studies on the effect of X are not consistent.
Smith's analysis does not take account of ..., nor does she examine ...
The existing accounts fail to resolve the contradiction between X and Y.
Most studies of X have only been carried out in a small number of areas.
However, much of the research up to now has been descriptive in nature ...
The generalisability of much published research on this issue is problematic.
Research on the subject has been mostly restricted to limited comparisons of ...
However, few writers have been able to draw on any systematic research into ...
Short-term studies such as these do not necessarily show subtle changes over time ...
Although extensive research has been carried out on X, no single study exists which ...
However, these results were based upon data from over 30 years ago and it is unclear if ...
Recent attempts to understand X (e.g. Smith 1989; Jones 1992) pay too little attention to ...
The experimental data are rather controversial, and there is no general agreement about ...
However, all the previous X research was cross-sectional in design. Therefore, it is unclear if ...
Although there are many reports in the literature on the outcome of X, most are restricted to ...
Some evidence suggests that ..., although further work using X is required to confirm this finding.

The existing literature on X Most of the work carried out on X	fails to ... suffers from ... does not address ... lacks clarity regarding ... ignores the possibility that ... has not distinguished between X and Y in a systematic way.

Previous studies	have failed to	explore consider take account of	the impact of ... the reasons for ... the evidence for ... the ways in which ... the contexts in which ... several key aspects of ... the variable nature of ... other explanations for ... the complex nature of ... the potential impact of ... the social dimension of ... the dynamic aspects of ... the underlying causes of ... all the possible effects of ... demographic factors that ... the ethical implications of ... the important role played by ... the broader implications of how ... the unique complexities faced by ... the contextual factors that influence ...

Previous studies (of X) Most of these studies	have	mostly mainly largely typically generally predominantly	ignored ... examined ... focused on ... concentrated on ... been concerned with ...

Previous studies (of X) Most of these studies	have suffered from	small sample sizes. low response rates. confounding factors. multiple design flaws. an overemphasis on ... inconsistent definitions. inadequate sample sizes. poorly developed theory. serious sampling problems. experimental design errors. poor case control matching. inadequate research design. a lack of clarity in defining ... a high degree of sampling bias. lack of instrumental sensitivity. considerable design limitations. the use of poorly matched controls. a paucity of standardised measures. fundamental flaws in research design. lack of a strong theoretical framework. an over-reliance on self-report methodology. a restricted range of methodological approaches. shortcomings in the methods used to select cases. a lack of well-grounded theoretical considerations.

Previous studies (of X) Most of these studies	have suffered from	certain several serious various notable	methodological	flaws. limitations. drawbacks. weaknesses. shortcomings.

Previous studies (of X) Most of these studies	have	only involved ... only been carried out in ... only been undertaken using ... only provided weak evidence for ... been of poor quality. been limited in a number of ways. been limited to convenience samples. been limited to a small number of cases. generally been restricted to the analysis of ... mainly been restricted to epidemiological observations.

No previous study has	controlled for ... been large enough to ... completely eliminated ... distinguished between ... provided information on ... addressed the question of ... assessed the occurrence of ... used a dynamic measure of ... given sufficient consideration to ... employed time-series techniques for ... utilised verbal reports to examine the problem of ... used a method for analysing multiple factors related to ...

General reference to previous research or scholarship: highlighting negative outcomes

Previous studies have failed to	find show demonstrate	a link between ... any treatment effect. a correlation between ... a connection between ... significant differences in ... any convincing evidence of ... a causal relationship between ... any support for the X hypothesis. any significant advantages of using ... significant changes in health outcomes. reliable, repeatable therapeutic effects of ...

Recent studies have The research to date has	not been able to	establish ... confirm earlier ... determine whether ... show a link between ... duplicate these results. reproduce these findings. replicate these associations. rule out the possibility that ... provide robust evidence for ... detect an increase in the risk of ... confirm earlier findings showing ...

Indicating missing, weak, or contradictory evidence
Evidence for X has been mixed.
The evidence for X is in fact ambiguous.
There is contradictory evidence as to whether ...
To date, there has been no reliable evidence that ...
To date, studies investigating X have produced equivocal results.
There is conflicting evidence on the relationship between X and Y.
The evidence that X and Y are associated with Z is weak and inconclusive.
Whilst evidence is increasing that ..., a consistent empirical picture is missing.
Studies undertaken so far provide conflicting evidence concerning the impact of ...
However, conflicting results from studies suggest the need for new investigations that ...
Previous research findings into X have been inconsistent and contradictory (Smith, 1996; ...).
Some studies have shown the beneficial effects of X, but others have shown a deterioration in ...

To date, (however), there has been	no little	clear solid reliable clear-cut scientific definitive empirical convincing conclusive experimental	evidence that ...

Identifying a knowledge gap in the field of study
Much less is known about X.
It is still not known whether ...
The nature of X remains unclear.
Currently, there are no data on ...
What is less clear is the nature of ...
Very little is currently known about X in ...
Research to date has not yet determined ...
What is not yet clear is the impact of X on ...
There is still uncertainty, however, whether ...
The response of X to Y is not fully understood.
Causal factors leading to X remain speculative.
The neurobiological basis of X is poorly understood.
Little is known about X and it is not clear what factors ...
To date, only a limited number of Xs have been identified.
The mechanisms that underpin X are not fully understood.
Much uncertainty still exists about the relationship between ...
Our understanding of how X influences Y is notably underdeveloped.
The potential impacts of X have not previously been analysed and quantified.
This indicates a need to understand the various perceptions of X that exist among ...
It is now well established that ... However, the influence of X on Y has remained unclear.

However,	what is not yet	clear known understood	is whether ... is the role of ... is the effect of ... is the nature of ... is the importance of ... is the extent to which ... is the degree to which ... is the actual proportion of ... are the different stages of ... are the circumstances that ... is the actual relationship between ... is the relative importance of the factors that ...

What remains	unclear unknown	(, however,)	is why ... is how ... is precisely how ... is to what degree there exists ... is how different species are distributed in ... is how such policies and practices affect the ... is whether these two systems interact. is whether the two conditions are related. is whether this finding is a true representation. is whether these two factors operate independently.

However,	(exactly) how	X affects Y X inhibits Y X develops X is formed X acquires Y X damages Y X produces Y X increases Y X influences Y X benefits from Y X contributes to Y	remains unclear. has yet to be determined. remains poorly understood. is (still) not yet fully understood.

The extent to which	X affects Y X inhibits Y X applies to Y X influences Y X moderates Y X determines Y X is related to Y X plays a role in Y X benefits from Y X contributes to Y X changes during ... X presents a risk to Y X corresponds with Y X may be attributed to Y X has been successful in ... X can be extrapolated to ... the problem of X is facilitated by Y these findings have wider relevance lack of X is causally associated with Y	is (still) remains	unclear. unknown. unexplored. poorly understood.

However,	several a number of	key further critical essential additional important interesting unresolved unanswered fundamental	questions remain about	the role of ... the nature of ... the effects of ... the aftermath of ... the treatment for ... the development of ...

Stating the focus, aim, or argument of a short paper

In this paper, I argue that ...
This paper has four key aims. Firstly, ...
The central thesis of this paper is that ...
In the pages that follow, it will be argued that ...
In this essay, I attempt to defend the view that ...
Specifically, the following issues will be addressed:
Secondly, the study aims to assess the extent to which ...
In the pages that follow, the following questions will be addressed:

This paper	argues that ... gives an account of ... discusses the case of ... analyses the impact of ... attempts to show that ... contests the claim that ... provides an overview of ... reviews the evidence for ... reports on a study which ... addresses the question of ... presents new evidence for ... traces the development of ... explores the ways in which ... assesses the significance of ... highlights the importance of ... considers the implications of ... evaluates the effectiveness of ... critically examines the view that ... proposes a new methodology for ... surveys recent empirical studies on ... examines the relationship between ... compares the different ways in which ... offers a new model for understanding ... investigates the factors that determine ... describes the design and implementation of ... seeks to remedy these problems by analysing the literature of ...

The (primary) aim of this paper is to	explore the ... trace the history of ... assess the claim that ... review recent research into the ... explore the relationship between ... contribute to the understanding of ... provide empirical evidence for the claim that ... propose a conceptual theoretical framework based on ...

The aim of this paper is to	critically	analyse the effects of ... examine the claim that ... review the evidence for ... examine the ways in which ... review the different approaches used to ... evaluate the rationale behind X's theory of ... discuss the some of the prominent ideas which ...

Stating the aims of the current research (note frequent use of past tense)

The specific objective of this study was to ...
An objective of this study was to investigate ...
This study set out to investigate the usefulness of ...
The objectives of this research are to determine whether ...
This prospective study was designed to investigate the use of ...
The aim of this study was to develop a better understanding of ...
This study therefore set out to assess the effect of X ..., and the effect of ...
The main aim of this study is to investigate the differences between X and Y.
Part of the aim of this project was to develop software that is compatible with ...
There were two primary aims of this study: 1. To investigate ... 2. To ascertain ...
This study seeks to obtain data which will help to address these research gaps.
One purpose of this study was to assess the extent to which these factors were ...
The purpose of this investigation was to explore the relationship between X and Y.
The aim of this research project has therefore been to assess the doses and risks associated with ...

This study set out to	explore ... determine whether ... try and establish what ... better understand the ... find a new method for ... evaluate how effective ... assess the feasibility of ... test the hypothesis that ... explore the influence of ... clarify several aspects of ... investigate the impact of ... identify the predictors for ... develop an understanding of ... gain further understanding of ... compare the two ways of treating ... examine the relationship between ... evaluate a new method of measuring ... determine the predictive validity of the... understand the views and experiences of ... review in detail the available information on ... describe some of the more recent developments in ... shine new light on these debates through an examination of ...

The aim of The purpose of	this study	was to has been to	predict which ... establish whether ... determine whether ... develop a model for ... examine the effects of ... assess the extent to which ... explore the relationship between X and Y. identify the most important factors influencing ...

Stating purpose of the current research with reference to gaps or issues in the literature

The current study aimed to address these	questions using ... limitations in two ways. problems through the use of ... gaps in the existing literature by ... discrepancies and investigate the ... concerns through the development of ... challenges by identifying methods applicable to ... issues by reviewing the scientific and technical data ...

Stating the purpose of the thesis, dissertation, or research article (note use of present tense)
This thesis examines the way in which the ...
This dissertation seeks to explain the development of ...
This case study seeks to examine the changing nature of ...
The overall aim of this thesis is to review the evidence for ...
This thesis applies methods in parametric models to address ...
This article examines the emerging role of X in the context of ...
This paper systematically reviews the data for..., aiming to provide ...
This thesis intends to determine the extent to which ... and whether ...
This dissertation aims to unravel some of the mysteries surrounding ...
Drawing upon two strands of research into X, this paper attempts to ...

This paper This thesis	aims to seeks to	explore the role of ... develop a framework for ... investigate the impact of ... extend our understanding of ... identify and describe factors that ... provide a deeper understanding of ... compare the clinical performance of ... evaluate behavioural interventions in ... examine and explain the processes which ... better understand the relationship between ...

Setting out the research questions or hypotheses
The hypothesis that will be tested is that ...
The research questions in this study focused on ...
The central question in this dissertation asks how ...
Specifically, the following issues will be addressed: ...
The specific questions which drive the research are: ...
This research seeks to address the following questions:
The key research question of this study was whether or not ...
This study aimed to address the following research questions: ...
The study sought to answer the following specific research questions: ...
In particular, this dissertation will examine six main research questions: ...

Describing the research design and the methods used
Data for this study were collected using...
Five works will be examined, all of which ...
A mixed-method approach was employed using ...
This investigation takes the form of a case-study...
This study draws on two theoretical frameworks ...
Qualitative content analysis was used to examine ...
This study utilised clustering techniques to identify ...
Contemporary source material was used to examine ...
This study was exploratory and interpretative in nature.
This study uses a qualitative case study approach to investigate ...
The research data in this thesis are drawn from four main sources: ...
This study employed survey methodology to investigate the impact of ...
The approach to empirical research adopted for this study was one of ...
This dissertation follows a case-study design, with in-depth analysis of ...
By employing qualitative modes of enquiry, I attempt to illuminate the ...
Qualitative and quantitative research designs were adopted to provide ...
This study makes use of oral history interviews as well as archival sources.
Both qualitative and quantitative methods were used in this investigation.
A holistic approach is utilised, integrating X, Y and Z material to establish ...
The study was conducted in the form of a survey, with data being gathered via ...
This project uses interviews and participant-observation to produce an account of ...
The methodological approach taken in this study is a mixed methodology based on ...
A combination of quantitative and qualitative approaches was used in the data analysis.

This study This investigation	uses used utilised	recent survey existing archival historical empirical interview secondary qualitative time-series quantitative longitudinal retrospective observational cross-sectional	data (from X) to	assess ... explore ... analyse ... examine ... estimate ... determine ... investigate ...

Explaining the significance of the current study

This is the first study to ...
This work will generate fresh insights into ...
Understanding the link between X and Y will help ...
The study should provide some important insights into ...
This is the first study to undertake a longitudinal analysis of ...
Investigating X is critically important in our understanding of ...
It is anticipated that findings from the project will help guide ...
The importance and originality of this study is that it explores ...
The present research explores, for the first time, the effects of ...
The findings should make an important contribution to the field of ....
It is hoped that this research will contribute to a deeper understanding of ...
This study aims to contribute to this growing area of research by exploring ...
This project provides an important opportunity to advance our understanding of ...
Therefore, this study makes a major contribution to research on X by demonstrating ...
There are several important areas where this study makes an original contribution to ...
The experimental work presented here provides one of the first investigations into how ...

This	study research investigation	sheds new light on ... provides new insights into ... fills a gap in the research on ... gives us new information on ... fills a gap in the literature by ... offers a fresh perspective on ... enhances our understanding of ... contributes to our knowledge of ... makes an important contribution by ... provides the first extensive examination of ...

The study presented	here in this thesis in this report	is one of the first investigations to	use ... utilise ... survey ... include ... explore ... employ ... compare ... undertake an ... examine in detail ... test the effects of ... focus specifically on ... assess the impact of ...

Giving reasons for personal interest in the research (sometimes found in the humanities, and the applied human sciences)

I became interested in Xs after reading ...
I have worked closely with X for many years and ...
This research complements an earlier study which ...
My personal experience of X has prompted this research.
My main reason for choosing this topic is personal interest.
The genesis of this thesis can be traced back to the time I spent ...
It is my experience of working with X that has driven this research.
This project was conceived during my time working for X. As a medical advisor, I witnessed ...

My (initial) interest in this area	began with ... arose when ... stemmed from ... was sparked by ... developed while I was ...

Explaining keywords (also refer to *Defining Terms*)

Throughout this paper, the term 'X' will refer to ...
The term 'X' will be used in this thesis to refer to ...
Historically, the term 'X' has been used to describe ...
This study utilises the concept of 'X' first proposed by ...
It is necessary here to clarify exactly what is meant by ...
The phrase 'X' will be used in this study to describe the ...
According to Smith (2002), X can be defined as follows: ' ... '
In this article, the abbreviation XYZ will be used to refer to ...
Throughout this dissertation, the term 'X' will be used to refer to ...
The term 'X' is a relatively new name for ..., commonly referred to as ...
In this essay, the term 'X' will be used in its broadest sense to refer to all ...
In this dissertation, the terms 'X' and 'Y' are used interchangeably to mean ...
While a variety of definitions of the term 'X' have been suggested, this paper will use the definition first suggested by Smith (1968) who saw it as ...

Describing the limitations of the current study

The thesis does not engage with ...
It is not the task of this paper to examine ...
This study is unable to encompass the entire ...
Establishing X is beyond the scope of this study.
The analysis of X presented here is based solely on ...
It is beyond the scope of this study to examine the ...
A full discussion of X lies beyond the scope of this study.
The reader should bear in mind that the study is based on ...
Another potential problem is that the scope of my thesis may be too broad.
Due to practical constraints, this paper cannot provide a comprehensive review of...

Outlining the structure of a short paper
The first section of this paper will examine ...
This paper begins by ... It will then go on to ...
The essay has been organised in the following way: ...
The remaining part of the paper proceeds as follows: ...
The main issues addressed in this paper are: a), b) and c).
This paper first gives a brief overview of the recent history of X.
This paper has been divided into four parts. The first part deals with ...

Outlining the structure of a thesis or dissertation
This thesis is composed of four themed chapters.
The overall structure of the study takes the form of six chapters.
The thesis is divided into three distinct sections. The first section ...
The third chapter is concerned with the methodology employed for this study.
Chapter 2 will consider both the sources and methods of study which will include ...
The purpose of the final chapter is to reflect on the extent to which this study has ...
Chapter 4 analyses the data gathered and addresses each of the research questions in turn.
Chapter 5 analyses the results of interviews and focus group discussions undertaken during ...
The fifth section presents the findings of the research, focusing on the three key themes that ...
Chapter Two begins by laying out the theoretical dimensions of the research, and looks at how ...

The second part The final chapter The final section	examines ... focuses on ... gives a brief review of ... contextualises the research by ... discusses the significant findings. draws upon the entire thesis to ... identifies areas for further research. ties together the common themes and ... explains the emergent themes influencing ... draws together these various findings, and ... draws together the key findings, making the ... draws together the various strands of the thesis. gives a brief summary and critique of the findings. summarises the main findings of this project and ... summarises the principal findings of these experiments and ... brings together the lessons from these case studies, and then ... describes the experimental approach and instrumentation utilised in ... ties together the various theoretical and empirical strands in order to ... includes a discussion of the implication of the findings to future research ...

Previewing a chapter

The aim of the chapter is to introduce ...
This chapter seeks to assess the impact of ...
This chapter is subdivided into three sections.
The first section will attempt to assess whether ...
The second part highlights the key theoretical concepts which ...
The following chapter contextualises the research by providing background information on ...
The next chapter discusses the specific methods by which the research and analyses were conducted.

The main	topics issues themes periods developments	covered in this chapter are ...

Reviewing the Literature

One of the distinguishing features of academic writing is that it is informed by what is already known, what work has been done before, and/or what ideas and models have already been developed. Thus, in academic texts, writers frequently make reference to other studies and to the work of other authors. It is important that writers guide their readers through this literature. This section of *Academic Phrasebank* lists some of the phrases that writers may use for this purpose.

A note on the literature review: It is the purpose of the literature review section of a paper or dissertation to show the reader, in a systematic way, what is already known about the research topic as a whole, and to outline the key ideas and theories that help us to understand this. As well as being systematic, the review should be evaluative and critical of the studies or ideas which are relevant to the current work. For example, you may think a particular study did not investigate some important aspect of the area you are researching, that the author(s) failed to notice a weakness in their methods, or that their conclusion is not well-supported (refer to *Being Critical*).

A note on referencing style: The way a writer refers to other sources varies somewhat across different disciplines. In some cases, where the individual author is important, the author's name will be the main subject of the sentence; in other cases, the author's name may only be mentioned in brackets (...) or via a number notation system (e.g. footnotes and endnotes). The 'author as subject' style is less common in the empirical disciplines (sciences) and more commonly used in the humanities. Different referencing systems are used in different disciplines. In the majority of the examples given here, the Harvard in-text referencing system has been used.

A note on verb tenses: For general reference to the literature, the present perfect tense (have/has + verb participle) tends to be used. For reference to specific studies carried out in the past, the simple past tense is most commonly used. This is normally the case where a specific date or point in time in the past forms a part of the sentence. When referring to the words or ideas of writers, the present tense is often used if the ideas are still relevant, even if the author is no longer alive. The examples given below reflect these general patterns, but these are by no means rigid.

General comments on the relevant literature

The literature on X has highlighted several ...
Much of the literature concerns X rather than Y.
Different theories exist in the literature regarding ...
More recent attention has focused on the provision of ...
There are relatively few historical studies in the area of ...
A great deal of previous research into X has focused on ...
A large and growing body of literature has investigated ...
Much of the literature since the mid-1990s emphasises the ...
Much of the current literature on X pays particular attention to ...
There is a large volume of published studies describing the role of ...
There is a relatively small body of literature that is concerned with ...
The existing literature on X is extensive and focuses particularly on ...
The generalisability of much published research on this issue is problematic.
A considerable amount of literature has been published on X. These studies ...
What we know about X is largely based upon empirical studies that investigate how ...
The academic literature on X has revealed the emergence of several contrasting themes.

Much of The greater part of	the literature on X	ignores ... focuses on ... is descriptive. comes from ... acknowledges ... takes as its focus ... is concerned with ... is exploratory in nature. lacks clarity regarding ... pays particular attention to ... seems to have been based on ... has emphasised the importance of ... perpetuates out-of-date notions of ... is extensive and focuses particularly on ...

Previous research: a historical perspective
Research into X has a long history.
Over the past two decades, major advances in X have allowed ...
For many years, this phenomenon was surprisingly neglected by ...
Only in the past ten years have studies of X directly addressed how ...
Prior to the work of Smith (1983), the role of X was largely unknown.
Early examples of research into X include ... (Smith, 1962; Jones, 1974).
Over the past decade, most research on X has emphasised the use of ...
In recent years, there has been an increasing amount of literature on ...
During the past 30 years, much more information has become available on ...
The first serious discussions and analyses of X emerged during the 1970s with ...
Historically, research investigating the factors associated with X has focused on ...
It is only since the work of Smith (2001) that the study of X has gained momentum.
An extensive series of randomised, controlled trials in the late 1970s demonstrated ...
The construct of X was first articulated by Smith (1977) and popularised in his book: ...
It was not until the late 1960s that historians considered X worthy of scholarly attention.
Awareness of X is not recent, having possibly first been described in the 5th century BCE by ...
Around the early 1960s, small-scale research and case studies began to emerge linking the use of ...

Previous research: area investigated as the sentence object
To date, several studies have investigated ...
A number of studies have begun to examine ...
Various studies have assessed the efficacy of ...
Researchers attempted to evaluate the impact of ...
A great deal of previous research into X has focused on ...
Several studies have used longitudinal data to examine ...
Previous studies have explored the relationships between X and Y.
Twenty cohort study analyses have examined the relationship between ...
A number of authors have considered the effects of ... (Smith, 2003; Jones, 2004).
At least 120 case-control studies worldwide have examined the relationship between ...
Numerous studies have attempted to explain ... (for example, Smith, 1996; Jones, 1998; ...).

To date, Thus far, Up to now,	several studies previous studies a number of studies	have	tested the efficacy of ... assessed the impact of ... investigated the effects of... begun to examine the use of ... aimed to determine whether ... used longitudinal data to examine ... examined the association between ... attempted to evaluate the impact of ... analysed the accuracy and precision of ... explored the relationships between X and Y.

Previous research: area investigated as the sentence subject

X has been proposed to explain how ...
The X problem has been extensively studied.
Xs have been studied extensively in vitro, using ...
X has been intensively investigated recently due to its ...
Markers for the prediction of X have been widely investigated.
X has also been shown to reverse the anti-inflammatory effects of Y in ...
These effects have been shown in X (e.g., Smith *et al.*, 1981; Jones, 1996).
Factors thought to be influencing X have been explored in several studies.
X appears to be positively related to both Y and Z (Smith, 2010; Jones, 2011).
The geology of X has been addressed in several small-scale investigations and ...
X has been identified as a major contributing factor to the decline of many species of ...
The roles of X have been studied extensively (Jones, 1989; Johnson, 1994; Smith, 1998).
The causes of X have been widely investigated (Jones, 1987; Johnson, 1990; Smith, 1994).
The relationship between X and Y has been widely investigated (Smith, 1985; Jones, 1987, ...

Previous research: approaches taken

Most research on X has been carried out in ...
Two different approaches have been used to ...
Most researchers investigating X have utilised ...
The majority of previous studies on X are based on ...
Using this approach, researchers have been able to ...
Several systematic reviews of X have been undertaken.
Historians have attempted to interpret X in the light of ...
The vast majority of studies on X have been quantitative.
What we know about X is largely based on observational studies.
Much of the previous research on X has been exploratory in nature.
There are a number of large cross-sectional studies which suggest ...
Much of the X research has focused on identifying and evaluating the ...
Traditionally, the study of X has been dominated by quantitative approaches.
Existing comparative studies are largely observational in nature, mostly relying on ...
Publications that concentrate on X more frequently adopt a historical or chronological approach ...

What we know about X is largely based upon	case clinical empirical qualitative simulation laboratory longitudinal comparative experimental observational epidemiological	studies that investigate how ...

(Most) recent studies have (Much of) the research to date has	been	conducted using ... carried out using ... largely exploratory. qualitative in nature. designed to determine whether ... based on relatively small sample sizes. undertaken in a variety of healthcare settings.

Previous research: what has been established or proposed
Several lines of evidence suggest that ...
Previous research has established that ...
Data from several studies suggest that ...
Recent evidence suggests that ... (Smith, 2019; ...).
It is now well established from a variety of studies that ...
New findings amongst X provides further evidence that ...
A number of studies have postulated a convergence between ...
Recently, considerable evidence has accumulated to show that ...
Surveys such as that conducted by Smith (1998) have shown that ...
Many recent studies (e.g. Smith, 2014; Jones, 2015) have shown that ...
Traditionally, it has been argued that ... (e.g. Smith, 1960; Jones, 1972).
Several biographies of Brown have been published. Smith (2016) presents ...
In previous studies on X, different variables have been found to be related to ...
Many historians have argued that ... (e.g. Jones, 1997; Brown, 1999; Smith, 2019).
There is a consensus among social scientists that ... (e.g. Smith, 2019; Jones, 2020; ...
Data from several sources have identified the increased X and Y associated with obesity.
Recently, in vitro studies have shown that X can ... (Smith *et al.*, 1997; Jones *et al.*, 1998).
It has been demonstrated that a high intake of X results in damage to ... (Smith, 1998; ...).
A series of papers on X (Jones, 1997; Brown, 1999; Smith, 2018) agree in suggesting that ...
Some cross-sectional studies suggest an association between X and Y (Smith, 2004; Jones, 2019).
There is a large number of published studies (e.g., Smith, 2015; ...) that describe the link between ...

It has been	noted that ... argued that ... shown that ... thought that ... assumed that ... reported that ... observed that ... suggested that ... established that ... demonstrated that .... conclusively shown that ...

To date, Thus far, Up to now,	several studies previous studies a number of studies	have	found ... reported ... shown that... linked X with Y. indicated that ... suggested that ... demonstrated that ... identified a link between ... confirmed the effectiveness of ... revealed a correlation between X and Y. highlighted factors that are associated with ...

Several Previous	studies of X surveys of X investigations of X	have	found ... shown ... revealed ... reported ... identified ... established ... demonstrated ... shown significant increases in ...

Stating what is currently known about the topic

X increases when ... (Smith, 2015)
X is able to affect Y (Smith, 2015; Jones, 2020).
X is positively related to Y (Smith, 2015; Jones, 2020).
X is proportional to Y as expressed by the... (Smith, 2015).
X is one of the most important ... (Smith, 2015; Jones, 2020).
X is one of the most intense reactions following Y (Jones, 2020).
A relationship exists between X and Y (Smith, 2015; Jones, 2020).
X is a principal determining factor of Y (Smith, 2015; Jones, 2020).
There is an unambiguous relationship between X and Y (Smith, 2015).
X is significantly reduced during the first months of ... (Smith, 2015; Jones, 2020).
X has been found to oppose the anti-inflammatory actions of Y on Z (Smith, 2019).

Previous research: highlighting negative outcomes

Previous studies have failed to	find show demonstrate	a (any) benefit in ... a (any) link between ... a (any) treatment effect. a (any) protective effect of ... a (any) correlation between ... a (any) connection between ... a (any) causal relationship between ... a (any) consistent association between ... a (any) statistically significant difference ... (any) convincing evidence of ... (any) benefits associated with ... (any) significant differences in ... (any) support for the X hypothesis. (any) significant advantages of using ... (any) significant changes in health outcomes ... (any) reliable, repeatable therapeutic effects of ...

Prior studies have Recent studies have The research to date has	not been able to	find ... detect ... confirm ... establish ... determine whether ... adequately control for ... convincingly show that ... reproduce these findings. account for all aspects of ... replicate these associations. confirm earlier findings showing ...

Reference to previous research: important studies

The first detailed study of X was ...
Smith (1960) was one of the first to examine ...
The first systematic study of X was reported by ...
Before Smith (1961), it was generally believed that ...
One of the most cited studies is that of Smith who sees ...
Smith (1952) helped to establish an explanatory model for ...
X is most commonly associated with the work of Jones (1960).
In one of the earliest studies in this field, Smith (1961) found ...
The first major fieldwork project that was undertaken in X was ...
The reaction between X and Y was first reported by Smith in 1872.
In their ground-breaking work in 1958, Smith and Jones established ...
A good summary of the classification of X has been provided in the work of ...
In a comprehensive literature review of X, Smith identified three significant ...
The electronic spectroscopy of X was first studied by Smith and Jones in 1970.
In 1985, Smith and Jones were the first of many investigators to demonstrate ...
X was first demonstrated experimentally by Pavlov (1927). In his seminal study ...
X formed the central focus of a study by Smith (2002) in which the author found ...
Perhaps the best-known study using this approach was carried out by Smith (1988).
One well-known study that is often cited in research on X is that of Smith (1972), who found ...
The way in which X is regulated was studied extensively by Smith and colleagues (Smith *et al.* 1995).
The innovative and seminal work of Smith pioneered a new approach to examining X and provided ...

By far Perhaps	the most	detailed thorough complete influential important well-known comprehensive widely accepted	account of X is to be found in the work of ...

Referring to a single investigation in the past: time prominent

In 1959, a seminal article was published entitled ...
Following this period, Smith actively searched for X.
In the 1950s, Smith pointed to some of the ways in which ...
Thirty years later, Smith (1974) reported three cases of X which ...
Almost 20 years ago, Jones (1995) formulated his X theory, centred around ...

In 1990,	Smith *et al.*	found that ... performed the first ... published a paper in which they described ... introduced a system of classification based on ... demonstrated that X induced in vitro resistance to ... reported a new and convenient synthetic procedure to ...

Referring to a single investigation in the past: investigation prominent
One longitudinal study found that ...
A seminal study in this area is the work of ...
One study by Smith (2014) examined the trend in ...
A recent study by Smith and Jones (2012) involved ...
A qualitative study by Smith (2003) described how ...
A recent systematic literature review concluded that ...
Preliminary work on X was undertaken by Jones (1992).
A longitudinal study of X by Smith (2012) reports that ...
A key study comparing X and Y is that of Smith (2010), in which ...
The first systematic study of X was reported by Smith *et al.* in 1986.
Detailed examination of X by Smith and Jones (1961) showed that ...
Analysis of the genes involved in X was first carried out by Smith *et al.* (1983).
A significant analysis and discussion on the subject was presented by Smith (1988).
The study of the structural behaviour of X was first carried out by Jones *et al.* (1986).
A small-scale study by Smith (2012) reached different conclusions, finding no increase in ...
The study by Jones (1990) offers probably the most comprehensive empirical analysis of ...

In an analysis of X, Smith *et al.* (2015) found ...
In a follow-up study, Smith *et al.* (2009) found that ...
In an investigation into X, Smith *et al.* (2012) found ...
In a study investigating X, Smith (2004) reported that ...
In a comprehensive study of X, Jones (2001) found that ...
In a study conducted by Smith (1998), it was shown that ...
In studies of rats given X, Smith and colleagues found that ...
In a study which set out to determine X, Smith (2012) found that ...
In a randomised controlled study of X, Smith (2012) reported that ...
In another major study, Smith (1974) found that just over half of the ...
In a recent cross-sectional study, Smith (2006b) investigated whether ...
In a large longitudinal study, Smith *et al.* (2012) investigated the incidence of X in Y.
In one well-known recent experiment, limits on X were found to be ... (Smith, 2019).

To examine this issue ... To better understand X, To compare the X with Y, ... To determine whether the ... To further examine the role of ... To further investigate the role of ...	Smith *et al.* (1990) carried out a series of experiments.

Using Taking	a(n)	historical integrated theoretical longitudinal evidence-based cross-sectional interdisciplinary intergenerational	approach, Smith (1990)	showed that ... demonstrated that ... was able to show that ...

Referring to a single investigation in the past: researcher prominent

Smith's comparative study (2017) found that ...
Jones's comprehensive review concluded that ...
Brown's (1998) model of X assumes three main ...
Smith's cross-country analysis (2017) showed that ...
Jones's (2010) review of the literature concluded that ...
Brown's (2022) recent analysis of X provides a strong critique of ...

Smith *et al.* (2018)	reported ... identified ... found that ... showed that ... demonstrated that ...
Jones (2018)	compared the rate of ... investigated whether ... calculated the average ... labelled these subsets as ... studied the effects of X on ... estimated the prevalence of ... measured both components of the ... used a survey to assess the various ... undertook a series of interviews with ... investigated the differential impact of... identified parents of disabled children as ... set up a series of virtual experiments using ... examined the flow of international students ... carried out a number of investigations into the ... analysed the data from 72 countries and concluded that ... interviewed 250 undergraduate students using semi-structured ... performed a similar series of experiments in the 1960s to show that ... reviewed the literature from the period and found little evidence for this ... conducted a series of trials in which he mixed X with different quantities of ...

Referring to important texts in the area of interest

With its publication in 1876, Smith's *XXXXX* established ...
In 1859, the publication of *XXXXX* had a major impact on ...
In his seminal text, *XXXXX*, Smith devoted some attention to ....
One of the most influential accounts of X comes from Smith (1986).
In Smith's landmark paper, *XXXXX* (1956), he adopted a Y approach to ...
One well-known early study, that is often cited in research on X, is that of ...
In her seminal paper entitled *XXXXX*, Smith (1981) identified problems with ...
Smith, in his comprehensive biography of X, devoted a substantial section to ...
Among the historiography of X, perhaps the most well-known work is that of ...
Herodotus, writing in the fifth century BC, provides the earliest description of ...
A more substantial approach to the longer-term significance of X can be found in ...
Smith *et al.,* in their book *XXXXX* (2006), give some reliable methods for calculating ...

Describing what other writers do in their published work

On the basis of these findings, Smith proposes that ...
In his analysis of X, Smith (2020) seeks to challenge ...
In Chapter 2, Smith provides us with a number of important ...
In the subsequent chapter, Smith examines the extent to which ...
By drawing on the concept of X, Smith has been able to show that ...
Some analysts (e.g. Jones, 2019) have attempted to draw fine distinctions between ...
In their recent review of X, Smith and Jones (2020) shed light on the new challenges in ...
Drawing on an extensive range of sources, the authors set out the different ways in which ...
Other authors (see Smith, 2016; Jones, 2019) question the usefulness of such an approach.

Smith (2019)	distinguishes ... cautions against ... calls our attention to ... stresses the role played by ... draws a distinction between ... builds on this earlier work by ... emphasises the importance of ... challenges the misconception that ... pinpoints a number of similarities between ... identifies X, Y, and Z as the major causes of ... draws on an extensive range of sources to assess ... traces the development of X during the 19th century. offers what may be the most complete treatment of ... highlights the need to break the link between X and Y. uses examples of these various techniques as evidence that ... mentions the special situation of Singapore as an example of ... lists three reasons why X has become so dominant. These are: ... draws our attention to distinctive categories of X often observed in ... discusses the challenges and strategies for facilitating and promoting ... questions whether mainstream schools are the best environment for ... considers whether countries work well on cross-border issues such as ... provides in-depth analysis of the work of Aristotle showing its relevance to ... defines evidence-based practice as the conscious, explicit and judicious use of ...

In her review of ..., In her major study, In her analysis of ..., In her seminal article, In her case study of ..., In her introduction to ..., In her classic critique of ..., In her historical account of ..., In her interesting analysis of ...,	Smith (2012) identifies five characteristics of ...

Referring to another writer's idea(s) or position

As argued by Smith (2003), X is far more cost effective, and therefore ...

According to Smith (2003), preventative medicine is far more cost effective, and therefore ...

Smith (2013)	claims argues suggests maintains concludes points out	that	preventative medicine is far more cost effective than ...

Jones (2013)	offers suggests proposes argues for makes the case for ...	an explanatory theory for ...

Synthesising sources: supporting evidence or ideas

Similarly, Jones (2015) found that X ...

This is consistent with the data obtained by ...

Smith (1995) makes a similar point in his study of X ...

In the same vein, Smith (1995) in his book XYZ notes ...

This view is supported by Jones (2015) who writes that ...

Along the same lines, Smith (1995) subsequently argued that ...

Smith argues that her data support Jones's (1995) view that ...

Jones's (1986) work on X is complemented by Smith's (2009) study of ...

Almost every paper that has been written on X includes a section relating to ...

A broadly similar point has also recently been made by Johnson (2019), who ...

Smith (2015)	sees X as ... argues that ...	Jones (2016), like Smith, maintains that ... Like Smith, Jones (2016) maintains that ... Similarly, Jones (2016) makes the case for ... Likewise, Jones (2016) holds the view that ... Supporting this view, Jones (2016) writes that ... Adopting a similar position, Jones (2016) argues that ... In the same vein, Jones (2016), in his book *XXXXX,* notes ...

Synthesising sources: contrasting evidence or ideas

Other writers have argued that ...
Other studies have concluded that ...
Unlike Smith, Jones (2013) argues that ...
In contrast to Smith, Jones (2013) argues that ...
Smith (2010) presents an X account, whilst Jones (2011) ...
While Smith (2008) focuses on X, Jones (2009) is more concerned with ...
A broader perspective has been adopted by Smith (213) who argues that ...
Contrary to previously published studies, Johnson *et al.* demonstrated the efficacy of...
This result conflicts with Smith's (1965) previously mentioned study which found that ...
Conversely, Smith (2010) reported no significant difference in mortality between X and Y.

Some writers (e.g. Smith, 2002) have attempted to draw distinctions between ...	Others (see Jones, 2003; Brown, 2004) question the usefulness of ...

Some authors have mainly been interested in questions concerning X (Smith, 2001; Jones ...)	Others have highlighted the relevance of ...

Whilst Smith identifies X as the principal dimension of Y,	Jones (2000) has taken a different approach by focusing on ...

Contrasting sources with 'however' for emphasis

Much of the available literature on X deals with the question of ...	However, Smith (2008) is much more concerned with ...

According to some studies, X is represented as ... (Smith, 2012; Davis, 2014)	However, others propose ... (Jones, 2014; Brown, 2015)

Smith (2013) found that X accounted for approximately 30% of Y.	Other researchers, however, who have looked at X, have found ... Jones (2010), for example, ...

Smith (2002) reports that ...	Jones's (2010) study of Y, however, found little evidence of ...

Unlike Smith,	(however),	Jones	accepts ... holds that ... thinks that ... insists that ... argues that ... suggests that ... sees great value in ... does not believe that ... embraces the idea that ... refuses to acknowledge ... provides a positive account of ... makes no distinction between ... acknowledges the role played by ...

Referring to secondary sources

Smith (1973, cited in Jones, 2010) points out that ...
Smith draws on the work of Jones (1959) who suggested that ...
Building on the work of Jones (2008), Smith (2012) argues that ...
Smith (2012) revisits and updates the Jones (1996) model of X by ...
Smith (2018, citing Jones, 2005) points out, X has been shown to result in ...
The view that ... is supported by Smith (2010) who draws on Jones's (1996) comparison of ...
Drawing on the work of a wide range of philosophers, Smith (2018) advances the notion that ...

Some ways of introducing quotations

Commenting on X, Smith (2003) argues: '... ...'
As Jones (2014: 215) states: 'there are many good reasons to be sceptical'.
As Smith argues: 'In the past, the purpose of education was to ...' (Smith, 2000:150).
In the final part of the *Theses on Feuerbach*, Marx writes: 'Philosophers have hitherto only ...'
Sachs concludes: 'The idea of development stands today like a ruin in ...' (Sachs, 1992a: 156).

As Smith	notes: '... ... ...' writes: '... ... ...' argues: '... ... ...' observes: '... ... ...' points out: '... ... ...' reminds us: '... ... ...'	(Smith 2013: 23).

Summarising the studies reviewed

Together, these studies indicate that ...
Overall, these studies highlight the need for ...
Considering all of this evidence, it seems that ...
Collectively, these studies outline a critical role for...
In all the studies reviewed here, X is recognised as ...
The evidence presented in this section suggests that ...
The studies presented thus far provide evidence that ...
Taken together, these studies support the notion that ...
Overall, there seems to be some evidence to indicate that ...
Together these studies provide important insights into the ...
All of the studies reviewed here support the hypothesis that ...
Two important themes emerge from the studies discussed so far:
However, such studies remain narrow in focus dealing only with ...
These research findings reported here consistently point towards ...
The evidence reviewed here seems to suggest a pertinent role for ...
These studies clearly indicate that there is a relationship between ...
In view of all that has been mentioned so far, one may suppose that ...
There remain several aspects of X about which relatively little is known.

Overall, these studies	suggest that ... suggest the efficacy of ... suggest an inverse association between ... suggest that the self-report method possesses ... suggest that both X and Y play a role in the development of ...
	illustrate how ... illustrate the role of ... illustrate the flexibility of ... illustrate the heterogeneity of ... illustrate just how important X is in ...
	highlight the need for ... highlight the complexity of ... highlight the positive aspects of ... highlight the beneficial effects of ... highlight the unique relationship between ...
	indicate a link between ... consistently indicate that ... clearly indicate the importance of ... indicate that Xs are often important predictors of ... indicate that the X has only a slight impact, if any, on ...

Overall, these studies	provide mixed evidence for ... provide converging evidence for ... provide strong evidence for the efficacy of ... provide clear evidence for the usefulness of ... provide reasonably consistent evidence of an association between ...
	show weak evidence of ... show that Xs may serve as important ... show a modest correlation between X and Y. show that X is caused by a complex system of ... show that a change from X to Y is usually associated with ...

Summarising the literature review
The previous section has shown that ...
In conclusion, these studies show that ...
The evidence reviewed here seems to suggest ...
To conclude this section, the literature identifies ...
From the studies reviewed here, it is evident that ...
This review has demonstrated the shortcomings of ...
In summary, it has been shown from this review that ...
Taken together, these studies support the notion that ...
In summary, little is known about the interrelationships between ...
This literature review points to the following general conclusions regarding ...
This section has attempted to provide a brief summary of the literature relating to ...

Describing Methods

In the Methods section of a dissertation or research article, writers give an account of how they carried out their research. The Methods section should be clear and detailed enough for another experienced person to repeat the research and reproduce the results. Where the methods chosen are new, unfamiliar or perhaps even controversial, or where the intended audience is from many disciplines, the Methods section will tend to be much more extensive. Typical textual functions found in this section of a research article or dissertation along with examples of the kind of language used for these are listed below. Note that, for many of the functional categories listed later in this section, the verbs are written in the simple past tense and are in the passive voice.

Describing previously used methods

Many researchers have utilised X to measure ...
One of the most well-known tools for assessing ...
Traditionally, X has been assessed by measuring ...
A number of techniques have been developed to ...
Different methods have been proposed to classify ...
X is the main non-invasive method used to determine ...
Different authors have measured X in a variety of ways.
Several methods currently exist for the measurement of X.
Previous studies have based their criteria for selection on ...
X is one of the most common procedures for determining ...
There are three main types of study design used to identify ...
The use of life story data has a relatively long tradition within X.
Recent advances in X methods have facilitated investigation of ...
There are a number of instruments available for measuring the ...
Recently, simpler and more rapid tests of X have been developed.
X and Y are currently the most popular methods for investigating ...
In most recent studies, X has been measured in four different ways.
The use of qualitative case studies is a well-established approach in ...
Xs have been used in the past to investigate the mechanical properties of ...
Case studies have been long established in X to present detailed analysis of ...
To date, various methods have been developed and introduced to measure X.
Since the 1950s, researchers have used a multitude of scientific methods to ...
This test is widely available and has been used in many investigational studies.
The methods for measuring X have varied somewhat across this research area.
In recent years, two different approaches have attempted to account for the ...
In recent years, molecular methods have been utilised for the quantification of ...
A variety of methods are used to assess X. Each has its advantages and drawbacks.
More recent examples of narrative studies within X can be found in the work of Smith (2010).
Two of the most common methods for estimating X are the use of Y and the measurement of Z.

X studies Studies of X	have traditionally	employed ... based their approaches on ... used model systems to predict ... adopted functionalist perspectives utilised a population-based approach. relied upon participant observation as ...

Various Different	methods have been	utilised to proposed to employed to	assess ... test for... identify ... capture ... quantify ... measure ... determine ... investigate ...

Indicating the methodology for the current research

The present study utilises X to analyse ...
The current study adopts a case study approach.
A qualitative methodology is employed in this study.
A mixed methods approach is employed in this research.
This investigation utilises energy analysis and statistical methods to ...
A participatory qualitative research approach is employed in this study.
The current investigation utilises an array of assessment techniques to ...
The current study uses qualitative analysis in order to gain insights into ...
It was decided that the best method to adopt for this investigation was to ...
This study employs qualitative analysis and natural language processing to ...

This study The current study	uses utilises employs	the X technique to ... archival research to ... an X methodology to ... the conceptual tools of ... a quasi-experimental design to ... experimental modal analysis to ... a descriptive research design to ... an ethnographic approach including ... a multi-method approach combining ... a qualitative research approach in which ... a randomised, double-blind trial involving ... critical discourse analysis (CDA) to examine ... interpretative phenomenological analysis to ... a qualitative methodology to critically evaluate how ... a mixture of quantitative and qualitative research methods to ... a cluster randomization design to examine the effectiveness of ...

Giving reasons why a particular method was adopted

A major advantage of X is that ...
The benefit of this approach is that ...
The decision to use X was based on ...
X based methods provide a means of ...
X was selected for its reliability and validity.
A case study approach was used to allow a ...
This method is particularly useful in studying ...
A quantitative approach was employed since ...
Qualitative methods offer an effective way of ...
The design of the questionnaires was based on ...
This approach is more suitable when the aim is to ...
The X method is one of the more practical ways of ...
The semi-structured approach was chosen because ...
The X approach has a number of attractive features: ...
The second advantage of using the multivariate method is ...
One advantage of the X analysis is that it avoids the problem of ...
Another advantage of using computer simulations is that it allows ...
Continuous sampling methods have a number of advantages over ...
The collaborative nature of the focus group offers another advantage ...
Qualitative methods can be more useful for identifying and characterising ...
The advantage of this particular method is that it allows us to make predictions about ...
Many of the distributions were not normal so non-parametric signed rank tests were run.
It was considered that quantitative measures would usefully supplement and extend the ...

A case study approach was	used chosen adopted	to ensure that ... to help understand how ... to allow a deeper insight into ... to conduct this exploratory study. to evaluate the effectiveness of ... to gain a detailed understanding of ... to determine the factors that affect ... to assess the management practices of ... to obtain further in-depth information on the ... to capture the complexities of the phenomenon. to provide rounded, detailed illustrations of the ...

X is one of the most	successful widely used commonly used	methods techniques	for	dating ... assessing ... gathering ... collecting ... evaluating ... estimating ... measuring ... identifying ... determining ...

A(n) The One	key major distinct obvious practical potential additional important significant	advantage	of using	Z-scores focus groups a rating scale secondary data self-report data longitudinal data retrospective data regression analysis natural speech data semi-structured interviews a convenience sample a case study approach a comparative approach a mixed method approach a multidimensional approach	is that ...

Referring to the literature to justify a method or approach

In a recent article, Smith (2009) argues that case studies offer ...
Smith (2020) has shown that this technique is very sensitive to ...
Smith *et al.* (1994) identify several advantages of the case study ...
Smith (2012) argues that case studies are useful when the conditions of the research ...
According to Smith (2011), semi-structured interviews have a wide-spread popularity in ...
The sensitivity of the X technique has been demonstrated in a report by Smith *et al.* (2011).
Smith (2006) points out that there is a role for both qualitative and quantitative approaches in ...

Indicating the use of an established method

The solution was then assayed for X using the Y method.
X was prepared according to the procedure used by Smith *et al.* (1990).
X was synthesised using the same method that was detailed for Y, using ...
Samples were analysed for X as previously reported by Smith *et al.* (2012).
Analysis was based on the conceptual framework proposed by Smith *et al.* (2002).
This compound was prepared by adapting the procedure used by Smith *et al.* (1990).
The questionnaire was adapted from that used by Smith *et al.* (1990) and included questions on ...

Giving reasons why a particular method was rejected

The limitation of this approach is that ...
A disadvantage of many cohort studies is that ...
A major problem with the experimental method is that ...
The main disadvantage of the experimental method is that ...
The principal limitation of the experimental approach is that ...
However, there are certain drawbacks associated with the use of ...
The disadvantage of this method is its reliance on the availability of ...
However, this method clearly is not valid for analysing long-term trends in ...
There are obvious difficulties in accepting the reliability of self-report information.
There are certain problems with the use of focus groups. One of these is that there is less ...

Explaining the provenance of the participants

A random sample of patients with X was recruited from ...
Forty-seven students studying X were recruited for this study.
The 5,880 study participants were recruited from four urban communities ...
The project used a convenience sample of 32 first year students studying at ....
The participants for this cohort were identified from a census questionnaire that ...
Participants were recruited from 15 clinics across X, covering urban and rural areas ...
Participants from X, Y, and Z were invited to complete a survey when they enrolled in ...
Potential participants who lived within the radius of the centre were invited to take part in...
A comparison group of 12 male subjects without any history of X was drawn from a pool of ...

Describing the characteristics of the participants

The cohort was divided into two groups according to ...
The sample was representative with respect to gender and ...
Just over half the sample (53%) was female, of whom 69% were ...
Of the initial cohort of 123 students, 66 were female and 57 male.
Eligible women who matched the selection criteria were identified by ...
Only children aged between 10 and 15 years were included in the study.
The participants were divided into two groups based on their performance on ...
Two groups of subjects were interviewed, namely X and Y. The first group was ...
All of the participants were aged between 18 and 19 at the beginning of the study...
The initial sample consisted of 200 students, 75 of whom belonged to minority groups.
All were between 18 and 30 years old (mean age = 24.27 years, s. d. = 2.05), and comprised ...
Semi-structured interviews were conducted with 17 male participants with a mean age of 38 years.

Explaining the provenance of articles for review

Literature was identified by searching ...
X was searched to uncover studies relating to ...
Additional searches were performed using the *Index of ...*
The small corpus of texts for this study was drawn from ...
Articles were searched from January 1965 to April 2014.
A systematic literature review was conducted of studies that ...
Electronic literature searches of X and Y were performed to identify ...
The literature was searched using electronic databases covering the period 2000–2008.

Indicating criteria for selection or inclusion in the study

Publications were only included in the analysis if...
To identify X, the following parameters were used: ...
Criteria for selecting the participants were as follows:
The area of study was chosen for its relatively small ...
Primary inclusion criteria for the X participants were ...
A number of criteria were considered when selecting ...
Eligibility criteria required individuals to have received ...
Five individuals were excluded from the study on the basis of ...
The inclusion/exclusion criteria for all participants were as follows:
The subjects were selected on the basis of the degree of homogeneity of their ...
All studies described as using some sort of X procedure were included in the analysis.
Articles were included if they reported a randomised, double-blind, placebo-controlled trial.

Describing the process: typical verbs in the passive form

All participants *were sent* ...
The data *were normalised* using ...
Ethical approval *was obtained from* ...
The drug *was administered by* ICV injection ...
Descriptive data *were generated for* all variables.
The procedures of this study *were approved* by ...
Prompts *were used as* an aid to question two so that ...
Data *were collected* using semi-structured interviews in ...
Participants *were thanked* for their time and effort and for ...
The experiments *were run* using custom software written in...
Two sets of anonymised questionnaires *were completed by* ...
A total of 256 samples *were taken from* 52 boreholes (Figure 11).
The solution *was washed* three times *with* deionized water and ...
Significance levels *were set at* the 1% level using the student t-test.
Data management and analysis *were performed* using SPSS 26.0 (2019).
Published studies *were identified* using a search strategy developed in ...
Data *were gathered* from multiple sources at various time points during ...
Injection solutions *were coded by* a colleague to reduce experimenter bias.
The pilot interviews *were conducted informally by* the trained interviewer ...
Article references *were searched* further for additional relevant publications.
The experiments *were conducted over* the course of the growing period from ...
Blood samples *were obtained with* consent, from 256 Caucasian male patients ...
The participants *were asked to* pay close attention to the characters whenever ...
Independent tests *were carried out on* the X and Y scores for the four years from ...
This experiment *was repeated under* conditions in which the signal/noise ratio was improved.
The mean scores for the trials *were subjected to* multivariate analysis of variance to determine ...

The participants were asked	to rate ... to recall ... to attend ... to record ... to indicate ... to memorise ... to say whether ... to comment on ... to complete two tasks. to answer a series of ... whether they believed ... to provide feedback on ... a variety of questions about ... to describe an instance when ... to explain what happened during ... to press the key corresponding to ... a series of open-ended questions that ... to describe what had happened when ... to complete a 20 question survey about ...

Describing the process: sequence words

To begin this process, ...
The first step in this process was to ...
The second method used to identify X involved ...

Prior to	commencing the study, ethical clearance was sought from ... analysing the interview data, the transcripts were checked for ... undertaking the investigation, ethical clearance was obtained from ... data collection, the participants received an explanation of the project.
(Immediately) After	'training', the participants were told that ... collection, the samples were shipped back to X in ... testing for the presence of antibodies, the blood was ... the appliance was fitted, the patients attended X every four weeks.
On	arrival at the clinic, patients were asked to ... completion of X, the process of parameter estimation was carried out. obtaining written informed consent from the patients, a questionnaire was ...
Once	the samples were extracted, it was first necessary to ... the Xs were located and marked, a thin clear plastic ruler ... the positions had been decided upon, the Xs were removed from each Y and ... the exposures were completed, the X was removed from the Y and placed in ...
Following	correction for ..., X was reduced to ... conformational analysis of X, it was necessary to ... administration of X to patients, we assessed the effects on ... this treatment, the samples were recovered and stored overnight at ...

The participants were	*then*	shown a film individually and were asked to ...
The soil was	*then*	weighed again, and this weight was recorded as ...
The preparation was	*then*	placed in a custom-built microfluidics chamber, covered with ...
These ratings were	*then*	made for the ten stimuli to which the subject had been exposed ...

When	dividing X, care was taken to ... removing X, it was important to ... inviting the participants, the purpose of the research was clearly explained.

Finally, questions were asked as to the role of ...
In the follow-up phase of the study, participants were asked ...
The final stage of the study comprised a semi-structured interview with participants who ...

Describing the process: *using* + instrument

All the work on the computer was carried out *using* ...
Data were collected *using* two high spectral resolution Xs.
Semi-automated genotyping was carried out *using* X software and ...
Qualitative data were collected *using* a semi-structured questionnaire.
Using the X-ray and looking at the actual X, it was possible to identify ...
Comparisons between the two groups were made *using* unrelated t-tests
The data were recorded on a digital audio recorder and transcribed *using* a ...
Statistical significance was analysed *using* analysis of variance and t-tests as appropriate..
15 subjects were recruited *using* email advertisements requesting healthy students from ...
The relationship between X and Y was examined *using* the Pearson correlation coefficient and ...

Describing the process: adverbs of manner

The resulting solution was	*gently*	mixed at room temperature for ...
A sample of the concentrate was then	*carefully*	injected into ...
The soil was then placed in a furnace and	*gradually*	heated up to ...
The vials were shaken	*manually*	to allow the soil to mix well with the water.
The medium was then	*aseptically*	transferred to a conical flask.
The tubes were	*accurately*	reweighed to six decimal places using ...

Describing the process: infinitive of purpose

In order to investigate the effects of ...
In order to identify ..., the participants were asked to ...
In order to help familiarise participants with ..., they were asked to ...
In order to address these ethical concerns, the following steps were taken: ...
In order to understand how X regulates Y, a series of transfections was performed.

To avoid ...
To test whether ...
To establish whether ...,
To better understand how ...
To address the possibility of ...
To measure X, a question asking ... was used.
To determine whether ..., the cells were incubated for ...
To rule out the possibility that ... , the participants were ...
To control for bias, measurements were carried out by another person.
To assess whether and how Xs are produced and received, we measured ...
To see if the two methods gave the same measurement, the data were plotted and ...
To compare the scores three weeks after initial screening, a global ANOVA F-test was used.
To enable the subjects to see the computer screen clearly, the laptop was configured with ...
To increase the reliability of measures, each X was tested twice with a 4-minute break between ...

The vials were capped with X *to prevent* ...
The process was repeated several times *in order to remove* ...
In an attempt *to make each interviewee feel* as comfortable as possible, the interviewer ...
The interview schedule comprised structured and open questions *to identify and explore* ...

Describing the process: expressing purpose with *for*

For the next two questions, a Likert scale was used.
For the purpose of analysis, two segments were extracted from each ...
For the purpose of height measurement, participants were asked to stand ...
For the estimation of protein concentration, 100 µL of protein sample was mixed with ...

Describing questionnaire design

The first question elicited information on ...
Seven questions, adapted from X, assessed ...
All survey questions utilised a 5-point Likert scale.
Using a 5-point Likert scale, participants were asked ...
A short questionnaire was designed to ascertain the participants' ...
The questionnaire was designed to measure the following constructs:
Participants were asked to respond using a 5-point Likert scale ranging from ...
The questions asked participants to rate how strongly they agreed with each statement.
The study began with two open-ended survey questions that asked participants to indicate ...
The questionnaire asked participants to complete three open-ended questions that asked about ...

The first question	was designed to	find out ... gauge how much... ascertain whether ... identify the types of ... test participants' knowledge of ... measure the students' ability to explain ... elicit a simple answer to a complex question about ...

Question 2 The third question The final question	asked participants	to list ... to rank ... to provide ... to describe ... to reflect on ... to choose between ... to indicate whether ... to rate how much they liked ...

Question 2 asked participants to indicate	whether ... which of three ... where and when ... the extent to which they ... what they liked best about ... how often they think about ... what their preferred X is for ... what percentage of the time ...

Q2 asked participants to rate	themselves as ... the intensity of ... their interest in ... the importance of ... their perception of ... the extent to which ... how frequently they ... their level of agreement with ... how strongly they agreed with the statement ...	on a 5-point Likert scale.

Describing the process: statistical procedures

The data *were normalised* using ...
A *p* value <0.05 *was considered* significant.
Descriptive data *were generated* for all variables.
Reliability *was calculated* using Cronbach's alpha.
All analyses *were carried out* using SPSS, version 26.
Non-parametric tests *were used* to compare the number of ...
Independent sample t-tests *were carried out* to assess whether ...
Statistical analysis *was performed* using SPSS software (version 26).
Significance levels *were set at* the 1% level using the student t-test.
Data management and analysis *were performed* using SPSS 26.0 (2019).
A Pearson correlation analysis *was conducted* in order to assess the strength of ...
An independent t-test was *carried out* on each of the variables to determine whether ...
The mean score for the two trials *was subjected* to multivariate analysis of variance to determine ...

An independent t-test was	run used conducted performed carried out	to	assess whether ... test the hypothesis that ... compare the mean scores of... determine whether there was a difference ... test for differences between the two groups. test whether any differences existed between ...

Indicating methodological problems or limitations

Several issues arose when collecting the ...
In particular, the analysis of X was problematic.
In observational studies, there is a potential for bias from ...
The small size of the dataset meant that it was not possible to ...
Further data collection is required to determine exactly how X affects Y.
Another major source of uncertainty is in the method used to calculate X.
In this investigation there are several sources for error. The main error is ...
It was not possible to investigate the significant relationships of X and Y further because...
The responses relating to X were subjective and were therefore susceptible to recall bias.

Reporting Results

The standard approach to this section of a research article or dissertation is to present and describe the results in a systematic and detailed way. When reporting qualitative results, the researcher will highlight and comment on the themes that emerge from the analysis. These comments will often be illustrated with excerpts from the raw data. In text based studies, this may comprise quotations from the primary sources. In quantitative studies, the results section is likely to consist of tables and figures, and writers comment on the significant data shown in these. This often takes the form of the location or summary statement, which identifies the table or figure and indicates its content, and a highlighting statement or statements, which point out and describe the relevant or significant data. All figures and tables should be numbered and given a title.

More elaborate commentary on the results is normally restricted to the Discussion section. In research articles, however, authors may comment extensively on their results as they are presented, and it is not uncommon for the Results section to be combined with the Discussion section under the heading: Results and Discussion.

Referring back to the research aims or procedures

The first set of questions aimed to ...
To compare the difference between ...
The purpose of Experiment 3 was to ...
Simple statistical analysis was used to ...
The next question asked the informants ...
To assess X, the Y questionnaire was used.
Changes in X and Y were compared using ...
The third research question was whether ...
Regression analysis was used to predict the ...
To distinguish between these two possibilities, ...
The first set of analyses examined the impact of ...
The correlation between X and Y was tested using ...
T-tests were used to analyse the relationship between ...
The average scores of X and Y were compared in order to ...
In order to assess Z, repeated-measures ANOVAs were used.
Nine items on the questionnaire measured the extent to which ...
To compare the scores three weeks after initial screening, a global ANOVA F-test was used.
The Pearson product moment correlation coefficient was used to determine the relationship ...

Transition: moving to the next result

If we now turn to ...
Further analysis shows that ...
Further statistical tests revealed ...
Further analysis of the data reveals ...
A comparison of the two results reveals ...
Turning now to the experimental evidence on ...
Comparing the two results, it can be seen that ...
The next section of the survey was concerned with ...
In the final part of the survey, respondents were asked ...

Referring to data in a table or chart

Table 1 Figure 1	shows displays presents provides compares	an overview of ... the experimental data on X. the summary statistics for ... the breakdown of X according to ... the median and range of scores for each group. the intercorrelations among the nine measures of X. the results obtained from the preliminary analysis of X. the scatter diagram of the relationship between X and Y.

As shown in Figure 1, As can be seen from the table (above), Looking at Figure 3, it is apparent that ... From the graph above we can see that ... It can be seen from the data in Table 1 that ...	the X group reported significantly more Y than ...

The table below illustrates The pie chart above shows The top half of the table shows The bottom half of the table shows	the proportion of different categories of ...

Means and standard deviations of X The results of the correlational analysis The themes identified in these responses The results obtained from the preliminary analysis of X	are shown are set out are displayed are presented are summarised can be seen can be compared	in Table 1. in Figure 1.

Highlighting significant data in a table or chart

What stands out in the table is ...
Closer inspection of the table shows ...
The X in Figure 2 is interesting because ...
It is apparent from this table that very few ...
The most interesting aspect of this graph is ...
In Fig.10 there is a clear trend of decreasing ...
What is striking about the figures in this table is ...
An inspection of the data in Table 1.5 reveals that ...
What is interesting about the data in this table is that ...
The figure above highlights the key difference between ...
The differences between X and Y are highlighted in Table 4.
From the chart, it can be seen that by far the greatest demand is for ...
From this data, we can see that Study 2 resulted in the lowest value of ...
This table is quite revealing in several ways. First, unlike the other tables ...
From the data in Figure 9, it is apparent that the length of time left between ...
Data from this table can be compared with the data in Table 4.6 which shows ...
As Table III shows, there is a significant difference (t = -2.15, p = 0.03) between the two groups.

What stands out in this	table chart figure	is the growth of ... is the high rate of ... is the dominance of ... is the wide range of ... is the rapid decrease in ... is the general pattern of ... is the difference between ... is the wide disparity between ... is the markedly lower rates of ...

Stating a positive result

The mean score for X was ...
An increase in X was detected.
A two-way ANOVA revealed that ...
Participants' ratings of X indicated ...
On average, Xs were shown to have ...
Strong evidence of X was found when ...
This result is significant at the p = 0.05 level.
The results, as shown in Table 1, indicate that ...
A positive correlation was found between X and Y.
Increasing the strength of X led to a reduction in ...
There was a significant positive correlation between ...
The difference between the X and Y groups was significant.
There was a significant difference between the two conditions ...
There were small but significant negative correlations between ...
A significant difference was found between X1 and X2, $t(11)$ = 2.906, p<0.01.
Respondents who reported low levels of X also reported significantly lower levels of Y.
There is a moderate correlation ($r2$ = 0.60, significant at less than 1% probability) between ...

Stating a negative result

No increase in X was detected.
No difference greater than X was observed.
No significant differences were found between ...
None of these differences were statistically significant.
No significant difference between the two groups was evident.
No significant reduction in X was found compared with placebo.
No evidence was found for non-linear associations between X and Y.
No significant correlation was found between X scores and the Y scores (p = .274)

X appeared to be unaffected by Y.
Only trace amounts of X were detected in ...
There was no evidence that X has an influence on ...
The results of this experiment show no clear-cut pattern of ...
The Chi-square test did not show any significant differences between ...
There was no significant difference between the groups with respect to ...
Overall, X did not affect males and females differently in these measures.
A clear benefit of X in the prevention of Y could not be identified in this analysis.
T-tests found no significant differences in mean scores on the X and Y subscales.

There was no	increase of X associated with ... significant difference between ... evidence that X has an influence on ... observed difference in the number of ...

No statistically significant	difference correlation	between the means was found. between the two groups was evident. was observed between X and Y groups. was found between X score and the Y scores. between the mean scores of these groups was evident.

Reporting positive and negative reactions

X occurred with successive increases in Y.
Increasing the strength of X led to a reduction in ...
With successive increases in intensity of the X, the Y moved further to ...
Following the addition of X, a significant increase ($p<0.05$) in the Y was recorded.

Combining X with Y did not produce ...
Stimulation of X with Y did not increase the ...
Different doses of X showed no measurable effect on ...
When X cells were stimulated with Y, no significant difference in Z was detected.

Highlighting interesting or surprising results

Of interest here is the increase in ...
Interestingly, the X was observed to ...
This result is somewhat counterintuitive.
Interestingly, this correlation is related to ...
The more surprising correlation is with the ...
Surprisingly, only a minority of respondents ...
The most surprising aspect of the data is in the ...
The correlation between X and Y is interesting because ...
The most striking result to emerge from the data is that ...
Interestingly, a significant interaction of X and Y was also observed.
It is worth noting that there were also differences in the ratios of ...
The single most striking observation to emerge from the data comparison was ...

This is a/an (rather)	surprising significant interesting remarkable unexpected disappointing	result. outcome.

One A further An important	issue theme factor problem concept category	that emerged	from the data was ... from the interviews was ... during the pilot interviews was ... at the initial stages of the analytic process was ...

Surveys and interviews: Reporting response rates

The overall response to the survey was poor.
Thirty-two individuals returned the questionnaires.
The response rate was 60% at six months and 56% at 12 months.
Of the study population, 90 subjects completed and returned the questionnaire.
Of 150 potential participants who were sent invitations, 80 agreed to take part in ...
By the end of the survey period, data had been collected from 64 individuals, 23 of whom were ...

There were 53 responses to the question: '...?'
Respondents were asked to indicate whether ...
The total number of responses for this question was ...
The overall response to this question was very positive.
Respondents were asked to suggest other reasons for ...
In response to the question: '...?', a range of responses was elicited.
This section of the questionnaire required respondents to give information on ...

Surveys and interviews: Reporting proportions

Over half of those surveyed reported that ...
A minority of participants (17%) indicated that ...
70% of those who were interviewed indicated that ....
Almost two-thirds of the participants (64%) said that ....
The majority of those who responded to this item felt that ...
When asked whether ..., 90% of the respondents reported that ...
Just over half of those who answered this question reported that ...
In response to Question 1, most of those surveyed indicated that ...
When the participants were asked ......, the majority commented that ...
Of the 148 patients who completed the questionnaire, just over half indicated that ...

Surveys and interviews: Reporting themes

Another reported problem was ...
Opinions differed as to whether ...
Concerns were expressed about ...
A number of issues were identified ...
A variety of perspectives were expressed ...
These views surfaced mainly in relation to ...
Concerns regarding X were more widespread.
There was a sense of X amongst interviewees.
Five broad themes emerged from the analysis.
A common view amongst interviewees was that ...
One concern expressed regarding X was whether ...
This theme came up for example in discussions of ...
The themes of X and Y recurred throughout the dataset.
Particularly revealing is how the participants described ...
Two discrete reasons emerged from this. First ... Second ...
Two divergent and often conflicting discourses emerged ...
Of the five themes, X was the most frequently coded theme in the data.
Issues related to X were not particularly prominent in the interview data.
The responses to Question 1 could be grouped into the following themes:
A recurrent theme in the interviews was a sense amongst interviewees that ...

Surveys and interviews: Introducing excerpts from interview data

As one interviewee said: '...'
As one interviewee put it: '...'
One informant reported that ...
The comment below illustrates ...
One participant commented: '...'
For example, one interviewee said: '...'
In one case, the participant thought that ...
Another interviewee, when asked ..., said: '...'
Other responses to this question included: '...'
Another interviewee alluded to the notion of ...
Talking about this issue an interviewee said: '...'
Commenting on X, one of the interviewees said ...
One individual stated that '...' And another commented '...'

Surveys and interviews: Reporting participants' views

It was suggested that ...
One interviewee argued that ...
There were some suggestions that ...
In all cases, the informants reported that ...
In their accounts of the events surrounding ...
There were some negative comments about ...
The participants on the whole demonstrated ...
Some felt that ..., while others considered that ...
Some interviewees argued that ..., while others ...
This view was echoed by another informant who ...
Whilst a minority mentioned that..., all agreed that...
Only a small number of respondents indicated that ...
A small number of those interviewed suggested that ....
For a small number of participants X was the reason for ...
Some participants elaborated further and explained that ...
The majority of participants agreed with the statement that ...
When asked about X, the participants were unanimous in the view that ...

One Some A few A number of The majority of A small number of The overwhelming majority of	informant(s) participant(s) interviewee(s)	felt that ... said that ... stated that ... argued that ... reported that ... indicated that ... proposed that ... remarked that ... suggested that ... commented that ... referred to ... emphasised ... attributed X to ... explicitly referred to ... questioned whether ... expressed a desire for ... were reluctant to discuss ... offered an explanation for ... expressed concerns about ... were particularly critical of ... agreed with the statement that ... welcomed the opportunity to focus on ...

Summarising the results section

These results suggest that ...
The results also indicate that ...
Overall, these results indicate that ...
In summary, these results show that ...
In summary, for the informants in this study, ...
What emerges from the results reported here is that ...
Together these results provide important insights into ...
Taken together, these results suggest that there is an association between ...
The results in this chapter indicate that ... The next chapter, therefore, moves on to discuss the ...

Discussing Findings

The term 'discussion' has a variety of meanings in English. In academic writing, however, it usually refers to two types of activity: a) considering both sides of an issue, or question before reaching a conclusion; b) considering the results of research and the implications of these. Discussion sections in dissertations and research articles are probably the most complex sections in terms of their elements. They normally centre around a 'statement of result' or an important 'finding'. As there is usually more than one result, discussion sections are often structured into a series of discussion cycles. The most common elements in these cycles, and some of the language that is typically associated with them, are listed below. Note that when offering explanations and suggesting implications the language used is very tentative or cautious (refer to the section entitled *Being Cautious*).

Providing background information: reference to the literature
A number of recent studies ...
Several reports have shown that ...
As mentioned in the literature review, ...
Prior studies that have noted the importance of ...
Very little was found in the literature on the question of ...
Previous studies evaluating X observed inconsistent results on whether ...
A strong relationship between X and Y has been reported in the literature.
In reviewing the literature, no data was found on the association between X and Y.

Providing background information: reference to the purpose of the study
One of the aims of this study was to ...
The third question in this research was ...
An initial objective of the project was to identify ...
This study set out to assess the importance of X in ...
The first question in this study sought to determine ...
It was hypothesised that participants with a history of ...
The present study was designed to determine the effect of ...
With respect to the first research question, it was found that ...

Restating a result or one of several results
This study found that ...
Another finding is that ...
The results of this study show that ...
The current investigation found that ...
In this study, Xs were found to cause ...
On the question of X, this study found that ...
The first part of the questionnaire revealed that ...
This experiment did not detect any evidence for ...
The most obvious finding to emerge from the analysis is that ...

Pointing out interesting or important findings
One interesting finding is ...
Another important finding is that ...
The most important result was that ...
Most striking was the substantial difference in ...
Another finding that stands out from the results reported earlier is ...

(Perhaps) the most	striking important disturbing significant interesting compelling unexpected clinically relevant	finding is ...

Indicating an unexpected outcome
What is surprising is that ...
Surprisingly, X was found to ...
One unanticipated result was that ...
What is curious about this result is that ...
Surprisingly, no differences were found in ...
This finding was unexpected and suggests that ...
One unexpected finding was the extent to which ...
It is somewhat surprising that no X was noted in this condition ...
The weak association of X with Y is interesting, but not surprising.
It is interesting to compare Figure 4 with Figure 2 in Smith (2019) that shows ...
One surprising variable that was found to be significantly associated with X was ...
These findings are somewhat surprising given the fact that other research shows ...
Contrary to expectations, this study did not find a significant difference between ...
However, the observed difference between X and Y in this study was not significant.
However, the ANOVA (one way) showed that these results were not statistically significant.
It was surprising that the X group scores did not differ significantly from those of the Y group.

Indicating an expected outcome
As might be expected, ...
It was not surprising to see that ...
This finding was not unexpected since ...
It is unsurprising that X was identified as ...
This is a relatively unsurprising finding given that ...
These findings are unsurprising, considering that ...
Unsurprisingly, the predicted impact of X increased when ...
The analysis of the effects of X on Y has, perhaps unsurprisingly, shown that ...

Comparing the result: supporting previous findings

This study confirms that X is associated with ...
Smith *et al.* (2015) reported similar effects when ...
This finding was also reported by Smith *et al.* (1998).
This finding is consistent with that of Smith (2000) who ...
Comparison of the findings with those of other studies confirms ...
This also accords with our earlier observations, which showed that ...
These results reflect those of Smith *et al.* (2015) who also found that ...
Increased activation in the X in this study corroborates these earlier findings.
These results corroborate the findings of a great deal of the previous work in ...
This finding broadly supports the work of other studies in this area linking X with Y.
In accordance with the present results, previous studies have demonstrated that ...
It is encouraging to compare this figure with that found by Smith (2015) who found that ...
Consistent with the literature, this research found that participants who reported using X also ...
There are similarities between the attitudes expressed by X in this study and those described by ...
This study supports evidence from clinical observations (e.g. Smith, 2007; Jones *et al.*, 2015) that ...

These results	further support the idea of ... confirm the association between ... are consistent with data obtained in ... match those observed in earlier studies. are in line with those of previous studies. are in agreement with those obtained by ... are in accord with recent studies indicating that ... agree with the findings of other studies, in which ... are consistent with those of other studies which found ... mirror those of the previous studies that have examined ... are consistent with those of Smith and Jones (2015) who ... are in keeping with previous observational studies, which ... support previous research into this area which links X and Y. are in agreement with Smith's (2015) findings which showed ... corroborate the ideas of Smith and Jones (2015), who suggested that ...

Comparing the result: contradicting previous findings

This study has been unable to demonstrate that ...
However, this result has not previously been described.
This outcome is contrary to that of Smith *et al.* (2020) who found ...
This finding is contrary to previous studies which have suggested that ...
In contrast to earlier findings, however, no evidence of X was detected.
The yields in this investigation were higher compared to those of other studies.
However, the findings of the current study do not support the previous research.
Smith *et al.* (1999) showed that .... This differs from the findings presented here ...
The overall level was found to be 15%, lower than that of previously reported levels.
It has been suggested that ... (Smith *et al.*, 2020). This does not appear to be the case.
The levels observed in this investigation are far below those observed by Smith *et al.* (2020).
These results differ from X's 2003 estimate of Y, but they are broadly consistent with earlier ...
Although, these results differ from some published studies (Smith, 2007; Jones, 2015), they are consistent with those of ...

Offering an explanation for the findings

A possible *explanation* for this might be that ...
Another possible *explanation* for this is that ...
This result may be *explained* by the fact that ...
There are, however, other possible *explanations*.
These relationships may partly be *explained* by ...
There are several possible *explanations* for this result.
Several factors could *explain* this observation. Firstly, ...
These differences can be *explained* in part by the proximity of X and Y.
A possible *explanation* for these results may be the lack of adequate ...
These factors may *explain* the relatively good correlation between X and Y.

This inconsistency may be due to ...
These results are likely to be related to ...
This discrepancy could be attributed to ...
It seems possible that these results are due to ...
This rather contradictory result may be due to ...
The observed increase in X could be attributed to ...
It is difficult to explain this result, but it might be related to ...
This finding could have been generated by misclassification bias since ...
Another possible alternative explanation of our findings is that they are due to ...

The possible interference of X cannot be ruled out.
It may be that these participants benefitted from ...
Differences between X and Y may have influenced ...
These possible sources of error could have affected ...
There are two likely causes for the differences between ...
This result may reflect differences in the size, quality and ...
The reason for this is not clear but it may have something to do with ...
The observed correlation between X and Y might be explained in this way: ...
Since this difference has not been found elsewhere it is probably not due to ...
These conflicting experimental results could be associated with the nature of the ...
It is possible that these unmeasured variables could account for some aspects of the results.

This (rather)	intriguing interesting surprising unexpected disappointing	result finding	could be due to ... may be related to ... might be a result of ... could be attributed to ... can be explained by X. might be explained by the fact that ...

Advising cautious interpretation of the findings

Another source of uncertainty is ...
Additional uncertainty arises from ...
A note of caution is due here since ...
We cannot exclude the possibility that ...
There are several possible sources of error.
Careful interpretation is needed here since ...
These findings cannot be extrapolated to all ...
These findings may be somewhat limited by ...
The possible interference of X cannot be ruled out.
These data must be interpreted with caution because ...
It could be argued that the positive results were due to ...
Several sources of error may have influenced these results.
These results therefore need to be interpreted with caution.
It is important to bear in mind the possible bias in these responses.
This limitation means that study findings need to be interpreted cautiously.
Although exclusion of X did not ..., these results should be interpreted with caution.
However, with a small sample size, caution must be applied, as the findings might not be ...

It is possible that these results	are due to ... are limited to ... are only valid for ... do not represent the ... have been confounded by ... may have been skewed by ... might be biased because of ... could be a statistical anomaly. were influenced by the lack of ... merely reflect a selection effect. may underestimate the role of ... are not a true representation of ... underestimate the true prevalence of ... might not be applicable to other groups ... are an artefact of our experimental design. are biased, given the self-reported nature of ... will not be reproducible on a wide scale across ... may not be generalisable to a broader range of ...

Commenting on the findings

This finding is reassuring since ...
These findings are rather disappointing.
However, these results were not very encouraging.
The test was successful as it was able to identify students who ...
The present results are significant in at least two major respects.
Unfortunately, these findings are rather difficult to interpret because ...

[illegible]	[illegible]g [illegible]ng [illegible]ant [illegible]cant [illegible]uring interesting remarkable encouraging disappointing	result(s). finding(s).

This is a These are	rather somewhat particularly	useful troubling surprising reassuring remarkable encouraging disappointing	result(s). finding(s).

Suggesting general hypotheses

These findings suggest that ...
It is possible, therefore, that ...
It can thus be suggested that ...
In general, therefore, it seems that ...
The findings reported here suggest that ...
According to these data, we can infer that ...
It is possible/likely/probable therefore that ...
The present study raises the possibility that ...
Hence, it could conceivably be hypothesised that ...
This observation may support the hypothesis that ...
It may be the case therefore that these variations ...
It is therefore likely that such connections exist between ...
The value of X suggests that a weak link may exist between ...
These results provide further support for the hypothesis that ...
Therefore, X could be a major factor, if not the only one, causing ...
It is possible to hypothesise that these conditions are less likely to occur in ...

Noting implications of the findings

These findings suggest that ...
It can therefore be assumed that the ...
This provides some explanation as to why ...
An implication of this is the possibility that ...
One of the issues that emerges from these findings is ...
These initial results are suggestive of a link between X and Y.
Some of the issues emerging from this finding relate specifically to ...
This combination of findings provides some support for the conceptual premise that ...

These	results findings	suggest that ... provide support for ... cast some doubt on ... have implications for ... support the idea that ... challenge the notion that ... might further indicate that ... may help us to understand ... may be taken to indicate that ... reveal something about the nature of ... are representative of an emerging trend in ... provide some tentative initial evidence that ... have important implications for developing ... may reflect differences in the size, quality and ... add to a growing body of evidence that suggests ... draw our attention to the importance of considering ... raise intriguing questions regarding the nature and extent of ... suggest that the lowering of X may reduce hospital admissions for ...

These findings	may will might should	help us to help others to	shape ... design... predict ... develop ... prioritise ... explain why ... find new ways of ... better understand ...

Suggestions for future work

This is an important issue for future research.
Research questions that could be asked include ...
Several questions remain unanswered at present.
Despite these promising results, questions remain.
There are still many unanswered questions about ...
Further work is required to establish the viability of...
These results warrant further investigation with a larger ...
Another potentially fruitful avenue for future research is ...
Further research should be undertaken to investigate the ...
A further study with more focus on X is therefore suggested.
There is abundant room for further progress in determining ...
Future studies on the current topic are therefore recommended.
In further research, the use of these data as X could be a means of ...
To develop a full picture of X additional studies will be needed that ...
In future investigations, it might be possible to use a different X in which ...
A comprehensive review based on more reliable study designs is recommended.
Further studies, which take these variables into account, will need to be undertaken.
However, more research on this topic needs to be undertaken before the association between X and Y is more clearly understood.

Further	work is research is studies are investigations are	needed to required to	identify the ... establish how ... confirm whether ... assess the risks of ... ascertain whether ... determine whether ... examine the effects of ... evaluate the impact of ... address the following questions: explore the mechanisms behind ... assess the longer-term impact of ... confirm and validate these findings. identify or develop drugs that can ... assess the competing therapies for ... develop reliable analytical methods for ... shed light on the mechanism underlying ... provide greater insight into the effects of ... gain a better understanding of the possible ... establish the effectiveness of treatment with ... better understand the mechanisms underlying ...

Writing Conclusions

Conclusions are shorter sections of academic texts which usually serve two functions. The first is to summarise and bring together the main areas covered in the writing, which might be called 'looking back'; and the second is to give a final comment or judgement on this. The final comment may also include making suggestions for improvement and speculating on future directions.

In dissertations and research papers, conclusions tend to be more complex and will also include sections on the significance of the findings and on recommendations for future work. In some research papers, the conclusion is not presented separately from the discussion section; the two sections may be combined. However, separate conclusions are nearly always expected for dissertations and essays.

Referring back to the purpose of the paper or study

This study set out to ...
This paper has argued that ...
This essay has discussed the reasons for ...
In this investigation, the aim was to assess ...
The aim of the present research was to examine ...
The purpose of the current study was to determine ...
The main goal of the current study was to determine ...
This project was undertaken to design ... and evaluate ...
The present study was designed to determine the effect of ...
The second aim of this study was to investigate the effects of ...
Returning to the question posed at the beginning of this study, it is now possible to state that ...

This study set out to	predict which ... establish whether ... determine whether ... develop a model for ... assess the effects of ... better understand the ... find a new method for ... evaluate how effective ... assess the feasibility of ... test the hypothesis that ... explore the influence of ... investigate the impact of ... gain a better understanding of ... objectively measure and assess ... examine the relationship between ... compare the two ways of treating ... critically examine the ways in which ... evaluate a new method of measuring ... provide the first systematic account of ... understand the views and experiences of ... review in detail the available information on ...

This study	has examined	the role of ... the impact of ... the nature of ... the concept of ... the differences between ... the relationship between ... the peer reviewed literature on ... the factors which are thought to contribute to ...

Summarising the main research findings
This study has identified ...
This study has shown that ...
The findings clearly indicate that ...
The research has also shown that ...
The second major finding was that ...
These experiments confirmed that ...
X made no significant difference to ...
This study has found that generally ...
The investigation of X has shown that ...
The results of this investigation show that ...
X, Y and Z emerged as reliable predictors of ...
Multiple regression analysis revealed that the ...
The most obvious finding to emerge from this study is that ...
The relevance of X is clearly supported by the current findings.
One of the more significant findings to emerge from this study is that ...

Suggesting implications for what is already known
In general, therefore, it seems that ...
The results of this study indicate that ...
The findings of this study suggest that ...
Taken together, these results suggest that ...
An implication of this is the possibility that ...
The evidence from this study suggests that ...
Overall, this study strengthens the idea that ...
The current data highlight the importance of ...
The findings of this research provide insights for ...
The results of this research support the idea that ...
These data suggest that X can be achieved through ...
The theoretical implications of these findings are unclear.
The principal theoretical implication of this study is that ...
This study has raised important questions about the nature of ...
The following conclusions can be drawn from the present study ...
Taken together, these findings suggest a role for X in promoting Y.
The findings of this investigation complement those of earlier studies.
These findings have significant implications for the understanding of how ...
Although this study focuses on X, the findings may well have a bearing on ...
These findings raised important theoretical issues that have a bearing on the ...

Explaining the significance of the findings or contribution of the study

The findings will be of interest to ...
This thesis has provided a deeper insight into ...
The findings reported here shed new light on ...
The understanding gained here should help to ...
The study contributes to our understanding of ...
These results add to the rapidly expanding field of ...
The contribution of this study has been to confirm ...
Before this study, evidence of X was purely anecdotal.
This project is the first comprehensive investigation of ...
The insights gained from this study may be of assistance to ...
This work contributes to existing knowledge of X by providing ...
This paper contributes to recent historical debates concerning ...
This is the largest study so far documenting a delayed onset of ...
Prior to this study it was difficult to make predictions about how ...
The analysis of X undertaken here, has extended our knowledge of ...
The empirical findings in this study provide a new understanding of ...
This is the first study which has examined the associations between ...
This approach will prove useful in expanding our understanding of how ...
By providing a conceptual model, this work offers a novel understanding of ...
This new understanding should help to improve predictions of the impact of ...
This is the first report on X from a nationally representative cohort of patients.
The methods used for this X may be applied to other Xs elsewhere in the world.
The X that we have identified therefore assists in our understanding of the role of ...
The findings from this study make several contributions to the current literature. First,...
These findings contribute in several ways to our understanding of X and provide a basis for ...

These findings	illustrate how ... could be used to help ... are important because ... are particularly relevant for ... provide insights into whether ... enhance our understanding of ... provide additional evidence for ... will help other researchers design ... highlight the potential usefulness of ... add to a growing body of literature on ... provide important insights into the role of ... provide strong empirical confirmation that ... represent a major breakthrough in the way ... make several contributions to the current literature. are relevant to both practitioners and policy makers. will be of use to the scientific and biomedical communities.

This study The present study The current investigation	has added to our knowledge of ... has extended our understanding of ... has given us a clearer understanding of ... has demonstrated, for the first time, that ... has provided a comprehensive assessment of ... has offered a framework for the exploration of ... has provided additional evidence with respect to ... has several practical applications. Firstly, it points to ... has been one of the first attempts to thoroughly examine ... has shed a contemporary light on the contentious issue of ... has gone some way towards enhancing our understanding of ... has confirmed the findings of Smith *et al.* (2001) which found that...

This is the first study	to identify ... to show that ... to investigate ... to test the effects of ... to firmly establish that ... to provide evidence for ... to reveal the presence of ... to investigate the effect of ... to use objective measures to ... to report an association between ... to integrate modelling approaches intended to ... that has used ... that has found ... that has revealed ... that has examined ... that has measured ... that has presented evidence for ... that has systematically analysed ... that has investigated the effects of ... that has documented the impact of ... that has evaluated the effectiveness of ... that has shown a clear-cut positive effect of ...

This investigation The present study The current research	is the first to compare the experiences of ... will serve as a base for future studies and ... should prove to be particularly valuable to ... makes several noteworthy contributions to ... lays the groundwork for future research into ... has provided a comprehensive assessment of ... provides the first comprehensive assessment of ... establishes a quantitative framework for detecting ... is the only empirical investigation into the impact of ... contributes to the growing body of research that indicates ... is important in furthering our understanding of the role of ... confirms previous findings and contributes additional evidence that ...

Prior to this	study, investigation,	X was unknown. it was difficult to ... there were no data on ... there was uncertainty about whether ... it had not been possible to determine ... no clear evidence of X had been reported. little was known about the characteristics of ... little evidence existed to support the idea that ... the influence of X on Y had not been thoroughly investigated.

Commenting on the strengths of the current study

A key strength of the present study was the ...
The main strength of this study is the exclusion of ...
One strength of this study is the high rate of follow-up, ...
The key strengths of this study are its long duration and ...
The strengths of the study included the in-depth analysis of ...
Although the findings should be interpreted with caution, this study has several strengths ...
One of the strengths of this study is that it represents a comprehensive examination of the whole ...

Introducing the limitations of the current study

A number of limitations need to be noted regarding the present study.
Study limitations make an overall conclusion about X extremely difficult.
The findings in this report are subject to at least three limitations. First, ...
Finally, a number of important weaknesses need to be considered. First, ...
With regard to the research methods, some limitations need to be acknowledged.
The generalisability of these results is subject to certain limitations. For instance, ...
Several limitations to this pilot study need to be acknowledged. The sample size is ...
The present study was subject to a number of potential methodological weaknesses.
The project was limited in several ways. First, the project used a convenience sample that
Although the study has successfully demonstrated that ..., it has certain limitations in terms of ...

Detailing specific limitations

A limitation of this study is that ...
Being limited to X, this study lacks ...
The major limitation of this study is the ...
The interference of X cannot be ruled out.
One issue with the current study was that ...
X makes these findings less generalisable to ...
Thirdly, the study did not evaluate the use of ...
X has meant that these findings are limited to ...
The generalisability of these findings is limited ...
It is unfortunate that the study did not include ...
The scope of this study was limited in terms of ...
However, these findings are limited by the use of ...
The most important limitation lies in the fact that ...
The main weakness of this study was the paucity of ...
Since the study was limited to X, it was not possible to ...
An additional uncontrolled factor is the possibility that ...
A limitation of using this kind of data is that it precludes ...
It was not possible to assess X; therefore, it is unknown if ...
An issue that was not addressed in this study was whether...
An arguable weakness is the lack of precision in our definition of ...
The study did not control for the possible confounding effects of ...
The principal limitation of this analysis was the variance in the design of ...
A potential source of bias for the study is the influence the researcher had upon ...
The responses relating to X were subjective and were therefore susceptible to recall bias.
The sample was nationally representative of X but would tend to miss people who were ...
One source of weakness in this study which could have affected the measurements of X was ...
The lack of X in the sample adds further caution regarding the generalisability of these findings.
With a small sample size, caution must be applied, as the findings might not be transferable to ...

This The current The present	study research investigation	is limited by ... has only examined ... has not been able to establish ... has only considered the context of ... has not been able to confirm earlier ... was unable to analyse these variables. was not specifically designed to evaluate factors related to ...

The current study	is limited by	the absence of ... the possible effect of ... the small number of cases. the relatively small sample. the fact that it only surveyed ... by the fact that it was restricted to ...

However, these results may not be applicable to	all types of ... all situations. other species. patients who ... all clinical settings. the wider population. other groups within ... organisations which ...

Another source of uncertainty	is has been	the role of ... the estimate for ... the assumption that ... the variation of X over time. associated with changes in ... the possibility of measurement errors in ...

Acknowledging limitation(s) whilst stating a finding or contribution

Notwithstanding these limitations, the study suggests that ...
Whilst this study did not confirm X, it did partially substantiate ...
Despite its exploratory nature, this study offers some insight into ...
In spite of its limitations, the study certainly adds to our understanding of the ...
Notwithstanding the relatively limited sample, this work offers valuable insights into ...
Although the current study is based on a small sample of participants, the findings suggest ...

Making recommendations for further research work

The question raised by this study is ...
The study should be repeated using ...
This would be a fruitful area for further work.
Several questions still remain to be answered.
A natural progression of this work is to analyse ...
More research using controlled trials is needed to ...
More broadly, research is also needed to determine ...
A further study could assess the long-term effects of ...
What is now needed is a cross-national study involving ...
Considerably more work will need to be done to determine ...
The precise mechanism of X in plants remains to be understood.
These findings provide the following insights for future research: ...
Large randomised controlled trials could provide more definitive evidence.
This research has thrown up many questions in need of further investigation.
A greater focus on X could produce interesting findings that account more for ...
The issue of X is an intriguing one which could be usefully explored in further research.
If the debate is to be moved forward, a better understanding of X needs to be developed.
I suggest that before X is introduced, a study similar to this one should be carried out on ...
More information on X would help us to establish a greater degree of accuracy on this matter.

Further	work needs to be done to establish whether ... studies need to be carried out in order to validate ... studies regarding the role of X would be worthwhile. experimental investigations are needed to estimate ... work is needed to fully understand the implications of ... research is required to establish the therapeutic efficiency of ... modelling work will have to be conducted in order to determine ... investigation and experimentation into X is strongly recommended. experiments, using a broader range of Xs, could shed more light on ... research in other Xs is, therefore, an essential next step in confirming ...

Further research	might explore ... could usefully explore how ... should focus on determining ... is required to determine whether ... in this field would be of great help in ... should be carried out to establish the ... should be undertaken to explore how ... on these questions would be a useful way of ... needs to examine more closely the links between X and Y. could also be conducted to determine the effectiveness of ...

More research	is needed is required	to account for ... in order to determine which ... to determine the efficacy and safety of ... to examine the long-term efficacy and safety of ... to better understand when implementation ends and ... to develop a deeper understanding of the relationships between ...

Further	research is studies are	needed required	to better understand	why ... how ... the nature of ... the causes of ... the impact of ... the reasons for ... the influence of ... the extent to which ... the role that X plays in ... how X is associated with ... the risks associated with ... the underlying causes of ... the possible link between ... the relationship between ... the discrepancies between ... the mechanisms underlying ... the effectiveness and safety of ... the complex linkages between ... the complex interaction between ... the complex association between ...

It would be interesting to assess the effects of ...
It is recommended that further research be undertaken in the following areas:
It would be interesting to compare experiences of individuals within the same ...
It is suggested that the association of these factors is investigated in future studies.

A *future* study investigating X would be very interesting.
In terms of directions for *future* research, further work could ...
In the *future*, it will be important to explore the potential use of ...
Another possible area of *future* research would be to investigate why ...
A number of possible *future* studies using the same experimental set up are apparent.
In terms of *future* work, it would be interesting to repeat the experiments described here using ...

Future studies should	include ... focus on ... target specific ... clarify whether ... attempt to identify ... assess the impact of ... explore the effects of ... seek to minimise bias by ... investigate the degree to which ... concentrate on the investigation of ... address the questions raised by this research.

Implications and/or recommendations for practice or policy

Other types of X could include: a), b) ...
Greater efforts are needed to ensure ...
There is, therefore, a definite need for ...
A second broad recommendation is that ...
Provision of X will enhance Y and reduce Z.
Management to enhance X might involve ...
Another important practical implication is that ...
Moreover, more X should be made available to ...
The challenge now is to fabricate Xs that contain ...
Unless governments adopt X, Y will not be attained.
These findings suggest several courses of action for ...
A reasonable approach to tackle this issue could be to ...
This particular research finding also points to the need for ...
Continued efforts are needed to make X more accessible to ...
These findings have implications within the clinical setting for ...
The findings of this study have a number of practical implications.
There are a number of important changes which need to be made.
This information can be used to develop targeted interventions aimed at ...
This study suggests that X should be avoided by people who are prone to ...
A key policy priority should therefore be to plan for the long-term care of ...
Taken together, these findings do not support strong recommendations to ...
Ensuring appropriate systems, services and support for X should be a priority for ...
The findings of this study have a number of important implications for future practice.
An implication of these findings is that both X and Y should be taken into account when ...

General Functions of Academic Writing

Being Cautious

One of the most noticeable stylistic aspects of academic communication is the tendency for writers to avoid expressing absolute certainty, where there may be a small degree of uncertainty, and to avoid making over-generalisations, where a small number of exceptions might exist. This means that there are many instances where the epistemological strength (strength of knowledge) of a statement or claim is mitigated (weakened) in some way. Writers may also wish to create a degree of distance between themselves and a statement or claim made by another writer. In the field of linguistics, devices for lessening the strength of a statement or for creating distance are known as hedging devices. Analysis of research reports have shown that discussion sections tend to be rich in hedging devices, particularly where writers are offering explanations for findings.

Devices that distance the writer from a proposition

It is thought that ...
It is believed that ...
It has been reported that ...
It is a widely held view that ...
It has commonly been assumed that ...

According to Smith (2002), ...
According to recent reports, ...
According to many in the field ...
Many scholars hold the view that ...
Smith (2001) is of the opinion that ...
Recent research has suggested that ...
If Smith's (2001) findings are accurate, ...
There is some evidence to suggest that ...
There is a growing body of evidence to suggest that ...

Being cautious when giving explanations

These frequent storms	may be could be might be are almost certainly	due to climate change.

It may be It is likely It could be It is possible It is probable It is almost certain	that	these frequent storms	are a result of climate change.

A likely explanation A possible explanation A probable explanation	is that	these frequent storms	are a result of climate change.

Being cautious when explaining results (Refer to: *Discussing Findings*)
This inconsistency may be due to ...
It is possible that this result is due to ...
This discrepancy could be attributed to ...
A possible explanation for this might be that ...
It seems possible that these results are due to ...
This rather contradictory result may be due to ...
The observed increase in X could be attributed to ...
There are several possible explanations for this result.
There are two likely causes for the differences between ...
A possible explanation for these results may be the lack of adequate ...
Since this difference has not been found elsewhere it is probably due to ...

Advising cautious interpretation of results (Refer to: *Discussing Findings*)
We cannot exclude the possibility that ...
These findings cannot be extrapolated to all ...
These findings may be somewhat limited by ...
The possible interference of X cannot be ruled out ...
These data must be interpreted with caution because ...
Several sources of error may have influenced these results.
These results therefore need to be interpreted with caution.
These results do not rule out the influence of other factors in ...
This account must be approached with some caution because ...
It is important to bear in mind the possible bias in these responses.
Although exclusion of X did not ..., these findings should be interpreted with caution.
However, with a small sample size, caution must be applied, as the findings might not be ...
The lack of a standardised measure makes it difficult to interpret these results with confidence.

It is possible that these results	may not apply to ... do not represent the ... do not accurately reflect ... have been confounded by ... may have been skewed by ... might be biased because of ... could be a statistical anomaly. might have been affected by ... were influenced by the lack of ... may underestimate the role of ... are not a true representation of ... underestimate the true prevalence of ... are an artefact of our experimental design.

Being cautious when discussing implications or recommendations

The findings of this study *suggest* that ...
Taken together, these results *suggest* that ...
The evidence from this study *suggests* that ...
These results would seem to *suggest* that the ...
These initial results are *suggestive* of a link between X and Y.
Initial observations *suggest* that there may be a link between ...
The findings from these studies *suggest* that X can have an effect on ...

One possible implication of this is that ...
Strategies to enhance X might involve ...
Other types of response could include: a) ..., b) ...
There would therefore seem to be a definite need for ...
A reasonable approach to tackle this issue could be to ...
The data reported here appear to support the assumption that ...
Another possible area of future research would be to investigate why ...

Being cautious when writing about the future

This phenomenon	may could might is likely to will probably will almost certainly	become more common in the future.

It is likely It is possible It is almost certain There is a possibility There is a small chance There is a strong possibility	that	the situation will improve in the long term.

Devices for avoiding over-generalisation: qualifying with *in general, generally*

In *general*, this requires ...
In *general* terms, this means ...
X is *generally* assumed to play a role in ...
Authors *generally* place an emphasis on ...
X uses *generally* accepted principles to ...
Generally accepted methods for X include: ...
Studies which show no effect are not *generally* published.
Research articles *generally* consist of the following components:
Quantitative research is *generally* associated with the positivist paradigm.

Devices for avoiding over-generalisation: using the words *tend, tendency*

In general, the study found a *tendency* for ...
There is a *tendency* for ozone to attack cells.
X *tends* to attack cells and break down tissues.
Smith (2015) found a *tendency* for X to be associated with ...
Smith *et al.* (1985) found a *tendency* for survey respondents to over-report ...
This results in a *tendency* for researchers not to venture beyond their own discipline.
The *tendency* for extreme scores to move toward the mean score over time is known as ...

Devices for avoiding over-generalisation: using qualifying phrases and adverbs

Ozone is toxic to	most almost all some types of many types of the majority of certain types of	living organisms.

Ozone levels	often generally frequently sometimes occasionally nearly always	exceed WHO levels in many cities.

Being Critical

As an academic writer, you are expected to be critical of the sources that you use. This essentially means questioning what you read and not necessarily agreeing with it just because the information has been published. Being critical also means looking for reasons why we should not just accept something as being correct or true. This can require you to identify problems with a writer's arguments or methods, or perhaps to refer to other people's criticisms of these. Constructive criticism goes beyond this by suggesting ways in which a piece of research or writing could be improved ... *being against is not enough. We also need to develop habits of constructive thinking.*[2]

Introductory phrases

Much of the criticism that X has attracted relates to ...
Critics question the ability of the X theory to provide ...
Many aspects of this interpretation have been questioned.
Non-government agencies are also very critical of the new policies.
Smith's meta-analysis has been subjected to considerable criticism.
A frequent criticism of much of the research on X concerns a general lack of ...
These claims have been strongly contested in recent years by a number of writers.
The X theory has been vigorously challenged in recent years by a number of writers.
More recent arguments against X have been summarised by Smith and Jones (1982).
Many analysts now argue that the strategy of X has not been successful. Jones (2003), for example, ...

Highlighting inadequacies of previous studies

Previous studies of X have not dealt with ...
Researchers have not treated X in much detail.
Such expositions are unsatisfactory because they ...
Most studies in the field of X have only focused on ...
Half of the studies evaluated failed to specify whether ...
The research to date has tended to focus on X rather than Y.
Most empirical studies of X have relied upon small sample sizes.
However, these studies used non-validated methods to measure ...
The vast majority of researchers have not considered the effects of ...
The existing accounts fail to resolve the contradiction between X and Y.
Most studies of X have only been carried out in a small number of areas.
However, much of the research up to now has been descriptive in nature.
Small sample sizes have been a serious limitation for many earlier studies.
The lack of reliable instruments is particularly problematic for studies of ...
None of the studies reviewed appear to have controlled for the effects of ...
The generalisability of much published research on this issue is problematic.
This general lack of methodological rigour may put in question the results of ...
However, few writers have been able to draw on any structured research into ...
There are obvious difficulties in accepting the reliability of self-report information.
However, these results were limited to X and are therefore not representative of ...
Most of the research on the association between X and Y is flawed methodologically.
The experimental data are rather controversial, and there is no general agreement about ...
Although extensive research has been carried out on X, no single study exists which adequately ...

---

[2] De Bono, E. (2016) *Parallel Thinking*. London: Ebury Publishing (p.58).

Most studies of X	have only focused on ... do not address the question of ... are unsatisfactory because they ... fail to estimate economic rates of ... have only investigated the impact of ... have not included variables relating to ... are limited by weak designs and a failure to address ... have only been carried out in a small number of areas.

Identifying a weakness in a single study or paper

We are not told how ...
The study suffers from ...
The paper fails to specify ...
No attempt has been made to ...
The study makes no attempt to ...
The article makes no reference to ...
The report provides little evidence that ...
A major problem with this experiment was that ...
No attempt was made to quantify the association between X and Y.
The scope of this research was relatively narrow, being primarily concerned with ...
Smith's study of X is considered to be the most important, but it does suffer from the fact that ...
However, these results were based upon data from over 30 years ago and it is unclear whether ...

The study	is limited	in that	it ignores ... it only considers ... it fails to provide ... it relies solely on ... it did not measure ... the sample is from ... it focuses solely on ... it investigates only one ... it does not take into account ... it did not assess frequency of ... the data collected come from ... it may be generalisable only to ... only 10 participants were included. it does not address the question of ... the definition of X did not encompass ... it does not clearly distinguish between ... it is a post-hoc analysis based on data gathered from ...

The research	is limited by	its reliance on ... the absence of ... incomplete data for ... the possible effect of ... the relatively small sample. the lack of information on ... the fact that it only surveyed ... the lack of clarity surrounding ... the generalisation of the term ... the fact that it only includes ... the fact that it is retrospective. the fact that it was restricted to ... the fact that there was no collection of ... the fact that it is cross-sectional in design. the fact that it relies on a questionnaire data to ... the fact that the participants self-reported their ... the fact that it only focused on the measurement of ... the fact that it does not account for variables such as ...

The paper	fails to does not makes no attempt to	specify ... quantify ... separate ... compare ... account for ... suggest why ... analyse how ... ascertain whether ... distinguish between ... explain the meaning of ... provide information on ... address the question of ... assess the effectiveness of ... use a standardised method of ... give sufficient consideration to ... consider the long term impact of ... offer an adequate explanation for ... engage with current discourses on ... determine the underlying causes of ... systematically review all the relevant literature.

(However,)	the study the paper	suffers from	selection bias. limited sample size. poor external validity. multiple design flaws. an overemphasis on ... serious statistical flaws. insufficient sample size. inconsistent definitions. poorly developed theory. historical and cultural bias. methodological limitations. serious sampling problems. a lack of clarity in defining ... inadequate research design. considerable design limitations. the use of poorly matched controls. a paucity of standardised measures. notable methodological weaknesses. fundamental flaws in research design. lack of a strong theoretical framework. certain ambiguities at the conceptual level. an over-reliance on self-report methodology. a restricted range of methodological approaches. shortcomings in the methods used to select cases. a lack of well-grounded theoretical considerations. several conceptual and methodological weaknesses.

However,	the analysis is largely superficial, based solely on ... the sample size in this study was relatively small ... this research has a number of methodological weaknesses. the degree of X experienced by patients was not measured. a major weakness with this study is that there was no control for X. a major problem with this experiment was that no control for X was used. the main methodological weakness is that X was only monitored for 12 months. one of the problems with the instrument the researchers used to measure X was ...

No attempt has been made to	estimate the risk of ... determine whether ... investigate whether ... quantify the degree of ... model the dynamics of ...

Introducing problems and limitations with a theory or argument

The main weakness with this theory is that ...
The key problem with this explanation is that ...
However, this theory does not fully explain why ...
One criticism of much of the literature on X is that ...
Critics question the ability of the X theory to provide ...
However, there is an inconsistency with this argument.
There are limits to how far the concept of X can be taken.
A serious weakness with this argument, however, is that ...
However, such explanations tend to overlook the fact that ...
One question that needs to be asked, however, is whether ...
One of the main difficulties with this line of reasoning is that ...
Smith's argument relies too heavily on qualitative analysis of ...
Smith's interpretation overlooks much of the historical research ...
Many writers have challenged Smith's claim on the grounds that ...
The X theory has been criticised for being based on weak evidence.
Smith's analysis does not take account of X, nor does he examine ...
The existing accounts fail to resolve the contradiction between X and Y.
It seems that Jones' understanding of the X framework is questionable.
Aspects of X's theory have been criticised at a number of different levels.
One of the limitations with this explanation is that it does not explain why... .
A final criticism of the theory of X is that it struggles to explain some aspects of ...
The X theory has been vigorously challenged in recent years by a number of writers.
A second criticism of the hypothesis draws upon research evidence which suggests ...
The X hypothesis has been questioned on the basis of some conflicting experimental findings.
Around the 1970s the consensus was that ..., but during the 1980s several researchers challenged this view.

The theory is unable to	predict ... explain why ... fully account for ... adequately explain the ... explain what happens when ... make any useful prediction about ... explain the differences observed when ... provide a comprehensive explanation for ...

The current model of X suffers from	poor scalability. unnecessary complexity. lack of empirical support. several methodological problems. certain weaknesses that hinder its ability to ...

Introducing problems and limitations with a method or practice

The limitation of this approach is that ...
A major problem with the X method is that ...
One major drawback of this approach is that ...
A criticism of this experimental design is that ...
The main limitation of this technique, however, is ...
Selection bias is another potential concern because ...
Perhaps the most serious disadvantage of this method is that ...
In recent years, however, this approach has been challenged by ...
Non-government agencies are also very critical of the new policies.
All the studies reviewed so far, however, suffer from the fact that ...
Critics of laboratory-based experiments contend that such studies ...
The disadvantage of this method is its reliance on the availability of ...
Another problem with this approach is that it fails to take X into account.
Difficulties arise, however, when an attempt is made to implement the policy.
There are obvious difficulties in accepting the reliability of self-report information.
Smith (2020) has identified a number of problems with the X approach. One is that ...
There are certain problems with the use of focus groups. One of these is that there is less ...
Critics have also argued that not only do surveys provide an inaccurate measure of X, but the ...
Nevertheless, the strategy has not escaped criticism from governments, agencies and academics.
Many analysts now argue that the strategy of X has not been successful. Jones (2003), for example, argues that ...

However, all the previously mentioned methods suffer from (some) serious	drawbacks. limitations. weaknesses. shortcomings. disadvantages.

However,	this method of analysis has a number of limitations. this method does involve potential measurement error. approaches of this kind carry with them various well-known limitations. questions have been raised about the reliability of self-report methods.

Selection bias is another (potential)	risk. concern. problem. limitation. weakness. threat to internal validity. limitation of systematic reviews.

Criticising an author or an author's work

Smith seems to ignore ...
Smith fails to grasp that ...
Smith's interpretation overlooks ...
Smith devotes insufficient attention to ...
Smith overlooks a number of important sources.
Smith fails to acknowledge the social aspects of ...
However, Smith's accounts are clearly ideological.
Although Smith has argued that ... she neglects to note that ...
Many aspects of Smith's interpretation have been questioned.
Smith's meta-analysis has been subjected to considerable criticism.
Smith's arguments for X have been forcefully questioned in recent years.
The most important of these criticisms is that Smith failed to note that ...
The most convincing rebuttal of Smith's interpretations has been written by ...
Smith's decision to prioritise X as the primary cause of Y has been widely attacked.
The scope of this research was relatively narrow, being primarily concerned with ...
Smith's study of X is considered to be the most important, but it does suffer from the fact that ...

Smith The book The paper	fails to does not makes no attempt to	specify ... quantify ... compare ... separate ... account for ... suggest why ... analyse how ... ascertain whether ... distinguish between ... explain the meaning of ... provide information on ... address the question of ... assess the effectiveness of ... use a standardised method of ... give sufficient consideration to ... consider the long term impact of ... offer an adequate explanation for ... engage with current discourses on ... determine the underlying causes of ... systematically review all the relevant literature.

Smith's paper	is	limited deficient problematic	in three areas. with regard to ... in two respects. in that it ignores ... in the sense that ... for several reasons.

(However,)	the paper does not address ... Smith fails to fully define what ... a major criticism of Smith's work is that ... Smith fails to acknowledge the significance of ... the author overlooks the fact that X contributes to Y. what Smith fails to do is to draw a distinction between ... Smith's paper would appear to be over ambitious in its claims. the main weakness of the study is the failure to address how ... another weakness is that we are given no explanation of how ... the research does not take into account pre-existing ... such as ... the study fails to consider the differing categories of damage that ... the author offers no explanation for the distinction between X and Y. Smith makes no attempt to differentiate between different types of X.

Smith The book The paper	overlooks fails to acknowledge makes no attempt to consider	the impact of ... the reasons for ... the evidence for ... the contexts in which ... several key aspects of ... the variable nature of ... other explanations for ... the complex nature of ... the potential impact of ... the social dimension of ... the dynamic aspects of ... the underlying causes of ... demographic factors that ... the ethical implications of ... the important role played by ... the broader implications of how ... the unique complexities faced by ... the contextual factors that influence ...

Offering constructive suggestions

The study would have been more interesting if it had included ...
These studies would have been more useful if they had focused on ...
The study would have been more relevant if the researchers had asked ...
The questionnaire would have been more useful if it had asked participants about ...
The research would have been more relevant if a wider range of X had been explored.

The study The findings Smith's paper Her conclusions	would have been might have been	more much more far more	useful original relevant convincing interesting persuasive	if he/she had if the author had	used ... adopted... included ... provided ... considered ...

A more comprehensive study would include all the groups of ...
A better study would examine a large, randomly selected sample of societies with ...
A much more systematic approach would identify how X interacts with other variables that ...

Evaluating work positively

This article provides a valuable insight into ...
Overall, X's study is a powerful explanation of ...
Smith's conception of X has been credited with ...
Smith's 2015 study is particularly helpful owing to its ...
Smith's research is valuable for our understanding of ...
The first major fieldwork project that was started in X was ...
In his seminal text, *XXXXX*, Smith devoted some attention to ...
Smith's account of X provides us with a useful lens through which ...
One of the most influential accounts of X comes from Smith (1986) ...
Smith's synthesis remains one of the most comprehensive studies of ...
Smith makes an interesting contribution with regard to the impact of ...
In a well-designed and robust study, Smith (1998) examined data from ...
A good summary of the classification of X has been provided in the work of ...
The pioneering work of Smith remains crucial to our wider understanding of ...
The most comprehensive study of X during this period has been undertaken by ...
Smith, in his comprehensive two-volume biography of X, devoted a substantial section to ...
A more detailed analysis of the longer-term impact of X can be found in Smith's recent article in ...
Smith's study is of great significance as it marks the first attempt to assess the broader impact of ...

Smith (1990)	offers provides presents	a useful a detailed an original a thorough an insightful an extensive an interesting a contemporary a comprehensive	analysis of ...

<table>
<tr><td rowspan="2">In his
In her
In this</td><td rowspan="2">useful
timely
seminal
detailed
thorough
excellent
influential
important
innovative
pioneering
impressive
wide-ranging
comprehensive
ground-breaking</td><td rowspan="2">study (of X),
survey (of X),
analysis (of X),
examination (of X),
investigation (into X),</td><td rowspan="2">Smith (2019)</td><td>found ...
concluded that ...
was able to show ...</td></tr>
<tr><td>argues that ...
makes the case for ...
provides a valuable ...</td></tr>
</table>

Smith's	seminal landmark influential thoughtful innovative pioneering fascinating informative wide-ranging comprehensive ground-breaking	study analysis	provides a valuable insight into ... makes a valuable contribution with regard to ... remains crucial to our wider understanding of ... is of great significance as it marks the first attempt to ...

Introducing the critical responses of individual writers
Smith (2014) disputes this account of ...
Jones (2003) has also questioned why ...
However, Jones (2015) points out that ...
The author challenges the widely held view that ...
Smith (1999) takes issue with the contention that ...
The idea that ... was first challenged by Smith (1992).
Smith is critical of the tendency to compartmentalise X.
However, Smith (1967) questioned this hypothesis and ...
Smith (1980) broke with tradition by raising the question of ...
Jones (2003) has challenged some of Smith's conclusions, arguing that ...
Another major criticism of Smith's study, made by Jones (2003), is that ...
Jones (2003) is critical of the conclusions that Smith draws from his findings.
An alternative interpretation of the origins of X can be found in Smith (1976).
Jones (2003) is probably the best-known critic of the X theory. He argues that ...
In her discussion of X, Smith further criticises the ways in which some authors ...
Smith's decision to reject the classical explanation of X merits some discussion ...
In a recent article in *Academic Journal*, Smith (2014) questions the extent to which ...
The latter point has been devastatingly critiqued by Jones (2003), who argues that ...
A recently published article by Smith *et al.* (2011) casts doubt on Jones' assumption that ...
Other authors (see Smith, 2012; Jones, 2014) question the usefulness of such an approach.
Smith criticised Jones for his overly restrictive and selective definition of X which was limited to ...
Smith's analysis has been criticised by a number of writers. Jones (1993), for example, points out ...

Smith	criticises ... questions ... challenges ... is critical of ... casts doubt on ... points out that ... takes issue with... raises a number of questions about ...

Introducing a section of text which has a critical purpose

The section below The section that follows	critically	assesses examines	the idea that ... the view that ... the quality of ... the claim that ... the concept of ... the role played by ... the argument that ... Smith's analysis of ... the effectiveness of ... the current approaches to ...

Classifying and Listing

> When we classify things, we group and name them on the basis of something that they have in common. By doing this we can understand certain qualities and features which they share as a class. Classifying is also a way of understanding differences between things. In writing, classifying is often used as a way of introducing a reader to a new topic. Along with writing definitions, the function of classification may be used in the early part of an essay, or longer piece of writing. We list things when we want to treat and present a series of items or different pieces of information systematically. The order of a list may indicate ranked importance.

Classifying a topic
X can be classified into Xi and Xii.
X can be categorised into Xi, Xii and Xiii.
Several taxonomies for X have been developed ...
Different methods have been proposed to classify ...
X may be divided into several groups: a) ..., b) ..., c) ...
Generally, X provides two types of information: Xi and Xii.
It has become commonplace to distinguish 'Xi' from 'Xii' forms of X.
X is generally classified into two types: Xi, also known as ..., and Xii or ...
There are two basic approaches currently being adopted in research into X. One is ...
The theory distinguishes two different types of X, i.e. social X and semantic X (Smith, 2013).
The works of Smith fall under three headings: (1) dialogues and ..., (2) collections of facts, and (3) ...

X may be divided into	three main	classes. categories. sub-groups.

X may be classified	in terms of according to depending on on the basis of	Y	into Xi and Xii.

Specific classifications
Smith (2015) draws a distinction between ...
Smith (2006) categorised X as being a) ..., b) ..., or c) ...
Smith's (1980) typology of X is the one most widely used.
Smith (1987) distinguishes between systems that are a) ..., b) ..., or c) ...
A third method, proposed by Smith (2010), bases the classification on a ...
To better understand X, Smith (2011) classified Y into three distinct types using ...
In 1960, Smith developed a system of classification that can be used by clinicians to ...
In Smith's system, individuals are classified as belonging to upper or lower categories of ...
For Smith, X is of four kinds: (1) X which ...; (2) X which ...; (3) X which ...; and (4) X which ...
Smith's Taxonomy is a classification system used to define and distinguish different levels of ...
Smith and Jones (2003) argue that there are two broad categories of Y, which are: a) ..., and b) ...

In Smith's scheme, In the traditional system,	Xs	are were	grouped classified	in terms of ... on the basis of ... according to whether ...

Smith (1996) describes	four basic kinds of validity:	logical, content, criterion, and construct.

Smith and Jones (1966)	divided grouped classified	Xs	into two broad types: Xis and Xiis.

Smith's taxonomy is	used to classify ... a hierarchical model for classifying ... a well-known description of levels of ... a classification of learning objectives .... a widely acknowledged classification system useful for .... a multi-tiered model of classifying X according to different levels of ...

Commenting on a system of classification: positive or neutral

This system of classification	includes ... allows for ... is widely used in ... helps distinguish ... is useful because ... is very simple and ... provides a basis for ... has clinical relevance. was agreed upon after ... can vary depending on ... is still respected and used. is particularly well suited for ... has withstood the test of time. is a convenient way to describe ... has been broadened to include ... was developed for the purpose of ... is more scientific since it is based on ...

Commenting on a system of classification: negative

This system of classification	is misleading. is now out of date. can be problematic. is in need of revision. poses a problem for ... is not universally used. is somewhat arbitrary. is simplistic and arbitrary. is inherently problematic. has relevance only within ... has some clear deficiencies. has now been largely abandoned. has limited utility with respect to ... is obsolete and tends to be avoided.

Introducing lists
Xs have three basic functions. Firstly, they ... Secondly, they ...
This topic can best be treated under three headings: X, Y, and Z.
The key aspects of management can be listed as follows: X, Y, and Z.
There are two types of effect which result when a patient undergoes X. These are ...
The *Three Voices for Mass* is divided into six sections. These are: the *Kyrie, Gloria*, ...
There are three reasons why the English language has become so dominant. These are:
This section has been included for several reasons: it is ...; it illustrates ...; and it describes...
The disadvantages of the new approach can be discussed under three headings, which are: ...
During his tour of Britain, he visited the following industrial centres: Manchester, Leeds, and ...
The *Mass for Four Voices* consists of five movements, which are: the *Kyrie, Gloria, Credo, Sanctus*, and *Agnus Dei*.

Referring to other people's lists
Smith and Jones (2020) list X, Y and Z as the major causes of failure.
Smith (2020) lists the main features of X as follows: it is A; it is B; and it has C.
Smith (2020) argues that there are two broad categories of Y, which are: a) ... and b) ...
Smith (2020) suggests three conditions for X . Firstly, X should be ... Secondly, it needs to be...
For Aristotle, motion is of four kinds: (1) motion which ...; (2) motion which ...; (3) motion which ...; and (4) motion which...

Comparing and Contrasting

By understanding similarities and differences between two things, we can increase our understanding and learn more about both. This usually involves a process of analysis, in which we compare the specific parts as well as the whole. Comparison may also be a preliminary stage of evaluation. For example, by comparing specific aspects of A and B, we can decide which is more useful or valuable. Many paragraphs whose function is to compare or contrast will begin with an introductory sentence expressed in general terms.

Introducing differences

X differs from Y in terms of ...
X is different from Y in a number of respects.
X differs from Y in a number of important ways.
There are a number of important differences between X and Y.
Areas where significant differences have been found include X and Y.
In contrast to earlier findings, however, no evidence of X was detected.
A descriptive case study differs from an exploratory study in that it uses ...
Smith (2013) found dramatic differences in the rate of decline of X between Y and Z.
Women and men differ not only in physical attributes but also in the way in which they ...
The nervous systems of Xs are significantly different from those of Ys in several key respects.

Smith (2003)	found observed	clear minor major distinct notable only slight significant considerable	differences between X and Y.

One of the most	crucial salient marked striking notable obvious important significant prominent noticeable interesting fundamental widely reported	differences	between X and Y	is ...

Introducing similarities

X is comparable to Y in terms of ...
Both X and Y share a number of key features.
There are a number of similarities between X and Y.
The effects of X on human health are similar to those of Y.
Both X and Y generally take place in a 'safe environment'.
These results are similar to those reported by (Smith *et al.* 1999).
This definition is similar to that found in (Smith, 2001) who writes:
The return rate is similar to that of comparable studies (e.g. Smith *et al.* 1999).
The approach used in this investigation is similar to that used by other researchers.
Studies have compared Xs in humans and animals and found that they are essentially identical.

The mode of processing used by the right brain	is similar to that is comparable to that is comparable in complexity to that	used by the left brain.

Comparing within one sentence using subordinating adverbs

Oral societies tend to be more concerned with the present	while whereas	literate societies have a very definite awareness of the past.

While Whereas	oral societies tend to be more concerned with the present,	literate societies have a very definite awareness of the past.

Comparing within one sentence using prepositional phrases

In contrast to Compared with	people in oral cultures,	people in literate cultures organise their lives around clocks and calendars.

Comparing within one sentence using contrastive verbs

Smith's interpretation	differs from that contrasts with that is different from that	of Jones (2004) who argues that ...

Comparing within one sentence using comparative forms

Women are more/less accurate than men in tests of....
In the trial, women made more/fewer errors than men.
Women tend to have greater/less verbal fluency than men.
Women tend to perform better/worse than men on tests of...
Women are more/less likely than men to perform well in tests of ...
Women are faster/slower than men at certain precision manual tasks, such as ...
Women are more/less likely to suffer from X when the front part of the brain is damaged.
The part of the brain connecting the two hemispheres may be more/less extensive in women.

Women	may be more/less susceptible to X are more/less accurate in tests of X are more/less likely to perform well make more/fewer errors in tests of X tend to have greater/less verbal fluency tend to perform better/worse in tests of X	than men.

Indicating difference across two sentences

It is very difficult to manage without calendar time in literate societies.	By contrast, In contrast, On the other hand,	many people in oral societies do not know the calendar year of their birth.

According to some studies, X is represented as ... (Smith, 2012; Jones, 2014).	(In contrast,) others propose ... (Jones, 2014; Brown, 2015)

Smith (2015) found that X accounted for ...	Other researchers, however, who have looked at X, have found ... Jones (2019), for example, ...

Jones (2015) reports that ...	However, In contrast,	Smith's (2019) study of Y found ...

Indicating similarity across two sentences

Young children learning their first language need simplified input.	Similarly, Likewise, In the same way,	low level adult learners need graded input supplied in most cases by a teacher.

Smith (2015) sees X as ... Smith (2015) argues that ...	Similarly, Likewise, In the same vein,	Jones (2019) asserts that ... Jones (2019) holds the view that ... Jones (2019) in her book *XXXXX* notes ...

Defining Terms

In academic work, students are often expected to give definitions of key words and phrases in order to demonstrate to their tutors that they understand these terms properly. More generally, however, academic writers define terms so that their readers understand exactly what is meant when certain key terms are used. When important words are not clearly understood misinterpretation may result. In fact, many disagreements (academic, legal, diplomatic, personal) arise because of different interpretations of the same term. In academic teaching and writing, lecturers and their students often have to explore these differing interpretations before moving on to examine a topic in depth.

Introductory phrases

The term 'X' was first used by ...
The term 'X' can be traced back to ...
Previous studies mostly defined X as ...
The term 'X' was introduced by Smith in her ...
Historically, the term 'X' has been used to describe ...
It is necessary here to clarify exactly what is meant by ...
This shows a need to be explicit about exactly what is meant by the word 'X'.

Simple three-part definitions

A university is	an institution	where knowledge is produced and passed on to others.
Social Economics may be defined as	the branch of economics	[which is] concerned with the measurement, causes, and consequences of social problems.
Research may be defined as	a systematic process	which consists of three elements or components: (1) a question, problem, or hypothesis, (2) data, and (3) analysis and interpretation of data.
Education is	a form of learning	in which the knowledge, skills, or values of a group of people are transferred from one generation to the next.
A scientific theory can be defined as	an explanation of some aspect of the natural world	[which has been] confirmed by observation or experiment.
Braille is	a system	of touch reading and writing for blind people in which raised dots on paper represent letters.
Science is	the systematic study of	the structure and behaviour of the physical and natural world through observation and experiment.

General meanings or application of meanings

X can broadly be defined as ...
X can be loosely described as ...
X can be defined as ... It encompasses ...
In the literature, the term tends to be used to refer to ...
In broad terms, X can be defined as any stimulus that is ...
Whereas X refers to the operations of ..., Y refers to the ...
The broad use of the term 'X' is sometimes equated with ...
The term 'disease' refers to a biological event characterised by ...
Defined as ..., X is now considered a worldwide problem and is associated with ...

The term 'X'	refers to ... encompasses A), B), and C). has come to be used to refer to ... is generally understood to mean ... has been used to refer to situations in which ... carries certain connotations in some types of ... is a relatively new name for a Y, commonly referred to as ...

X is a/an	broad generic common umbrella non-specific relatively new	term	that refers to ... used to describe ... which encompasses ... covering a wide range of ...

Indicating varying definitions

The definition of X has evolved.
There are multiple definitions of X.
Several definitions of X have been proposed.
In the field of X, various definitions of X are found.
The term 'X' embodies a multitude of concepts which ...
This term has two overlapping, even slightly confusing meanings.
Widely varying definitions of X have emerged (Smith and Jones, 1999).
Despite its common usage, X is used in different disciplines to mean different things.
Since the definition of X varies among researchers, it is important to clarify how the term is used in ...

The meaning of this term	has evolved. has varied over time. has been extended to refer to ... has been broadened in recent years. has not been consistent throughout ... has changed somewhat from its original definition, particularly in ...

Indicating difficulties in defining a term

'X' is a contested term.
'X' is a rather nebulous term ...
X is challenging to define because ...
A precise definition of X has proved elusive.
A generally accepted definition of X is lacking.
Unfortunately, 'X' remains a poorly defined term.
There is no agreed definition on what constitutes ...
There is little consensus about what X actually means.
There is a degree of uncertainty around the terminology in ...
These terms are often used interchangeably and without precision.
Numerous terms are used to describe X, the most common of which are ....
The definition of X varies in the literature and there is terminological confusion.
Smith (2001) identified four abilities that might be subsumed under the term 'X': a) ...
'X' is a term frequently used in the literature, but to date there is no consensus about ...
X is a commonly used notion in psychology and yet it is a concept difficult to define precisely.
Although differences of opinion still exist, there appears to be some agreement that X refers to ...

The meaning of this term	has been disputed. has been debated ever since ... has proved to be notoriously hard to define. has been an object of major disagreement in ... has been a matter of ongoing discussion among ...

Referring to people's definitions: author prominent

For Smith (2015), X means ...
Smith (2015) uses the term 'X' to refer to ...
Smith (1954) was apparently the first to use the term ...
In 1987, psychologist John Smith popularized the term 'X' to describe ...
According to a definition provided by Smith (2015:23), X is 'the maximally ...
Smith, has shown that, as late as 1920, Jones was using the term 'X' to refer to particular ...
One of the first people to define nursing was Florence Nightingale (1860), who wrote: '... ...'
Chomsky writes that a grammar is a 'device of some sort for producing the ....' (1957, p.11).
Aristotle defines the imagination as 'the movement which results upon an actual sensation.'
Smith *et al.* (2015) have provided a new definition of health: 'health is a state of being with ...

Referring to people's definitions: author non-prominent

X is defined by Smith (2015: 119) as '... ...'
The term 'X' was introduced by Smith in her ...
The term 'X' is used by Smith (2015) to refer to ...
The terms 'X' and 'Y' were first used by Smith (1954).
X is, for Smith (2015), the situation which occurs when ...
A further definition is given by Smith (2015) who describes ...
This definition is close to that of Smith (2015) who defines X as ...
A similar definition has been proposed by Smith *et al.* (2015), who have argued that ...
The term 'X' is used by Aristotle in four overlapping senses. First, it is the underlying ...
X is the degree to which an assessment process or device measures ... (Smith *et al.*, 2015).

Commenting on a definition

This definition	includes ... allows for ... highlights the ... helps distinguish ... takes into account ... poses a problem for ... will continue to evolve. can vary depending on ... was agreed upon after ... is intended primarily for ... has largely fallen out of use. fails to capture the idea of ... raises some important issues. has been broadened to include ... captures a number of important features of ...

The following definition is	intended to ... modelled on ... too simplistic. useful because ... problematic as ... rather imprecise. inadequate since ... does not recognise ... in need of revision since ... important for what it excludes. the most precise produced so far.

What is	useful striking notable troubling appealing significant important distinctive interesting remarkable	about this definition is	that it offers ... that it stresses ... the emphasis on ... that it recognises ... that it is based on ... that it clearly links ... that it acknowledges ... that it encompasses all ... that it takes for granted ... what it does not include ...

Specifying terms that are used in an essay or thesis

The term 'X' is used here to refer to ...
In the present study, X is defined as ...
The term 'X' will be used solely when referring to ...
This study utilises the concept of X first proposed by ...
In this essay, the term 'X' will be used in its broadest sense to refer to all ...
In this paper, the term that will be used to describe this phenomenon is 'X'.
In this dissertation, the terms 'X' and 'Y' are used interchangeably to mean ...
Throughout this thesis, I use the term 'X' to refer to informal systems as well as ...
While a variety of definitions of the term 'X' have been suggested, this paper will use the definition first suggested by Smith (1968) who saw it as ...

Describing Trends and Projections

A trend is the general direction in which something is developing or changing over time. A projection is a prediction of future change. Trends and projections are usually illustrated using line graphs in which the horizontal axis represents time. Some of the language commonly used for writing about trends and projections is given below.

Describing trends

Figure 2 The graph	shows that there has been a	slight steep sharp steady gradual marked	fall rise drop decline increase decrease	in the number of ....

Highlighting a trend in a table or chart

What is striking What stands out What is interesting What can be clearly seen	in this	table chart figure	is the rise in ... is the growth of ... is the increase in ... is the variability of ... is the dominance of ... is the high rate of ... is the rapid decrease in ... is the steady decline of ... is the general pattern of ... is the dramatic decline in ... is the continual growth of ... is the phenomenal growth of ... is the marked difference between ...

Describing high and low points in figures
Production of X peaked in 1985.
X rose to a high point and peaked in ...
The peak age for committing a crime is 18.
The number of Xs reached a peak during ...

Production of X reached a low point in 2015.
The rate fell to a low point of $5.00 at the end of the year.

Projecting trends

The rate of X The amount of X The number of Ys	is likely to will probably is expected to is projected to is anticipated to	fall reach ... rise to ... increase level off decline by ... drop sharply remain steady be as high as ... decline steadily continue decreasing grow by more than ...	after 2035.

Describing Quantities

The language for writing about quantities can be a complex area for non-native speakers because there are many combinations of short grammar words, such as prepositions and pronouns, and these can easily be confused. Many of the phrases given below also contain approximators such as: *nearly, approximately, over half, less than, just over.*

Describing fractions and percentages

Over half of those surveyed indicated that ...
Nearly half of the respondents (48%) agreed that ...
Almost two-thirds of the participants (64%) said that ....
Approximately half of those surveyed did not comment on ...
Of the 270 participants, *nearly one-third* did not agree about ...
Less than a third of those who responded (32%) indicated that ...
The number of cases in the United Kingdom fell *by nearly two-fifths.*
Of the 148 participants who completed the questionnaire, *just over half* indicated that ...

The incidence of X has been estimated *as 10%* ...
70% of those who were interviewed indicated that ...
Since 1981, England has experienced an *89% increase* in crime.
The response rate was *60% at six months and 56% at 12 months.*
Returned surveys from 34 radiologists yielded *a 34% response rate*.
He also noted that *fewer than 10% of* the articles included in his study cited ...
With each year of advancing age, the probability of having X *increased by 9.6%* (p = 0.006) is ...
The mean income of *the bottom 20 percent* of U.S. families declined from $10,716 in 1970 to ...

<table>
<tr><td rowspan="2">Just over
Well over
More than
Many more than

Almost
Around
Approximately

Just under
Less than
Fewer than
Well under</td><td>half
a third
a quarter</td><td rowspan="2">of those surveyed
of the respondents
of those who responded</td><td rowspan="2">agreed that ...
indicated that ...
did not respond to this question.</td></tr>
<tr><td>40%
50%
80%</td></tr>
</table>

Describing averages
The average of 12 observations in the X, Y and Z is 19.2 mgs/m ...
Roman slaves probably had a *lower than average life expectancy.*
This figure can be seen as the *average life expectancy* at various ages.
The proposed model suggests a steep decline *in mean life expectancy* ...
The *mean age of Xs with* coronary atherosclerosis was 48.3 ± 6.3 years.
The *mean estimated age at death* was 38.1 ± 12.0 years (ranging from 10 to 60+ years)
The *mean income* of the bottom 20 percent of U.S. families declined from $10,716 in 1970 to ...
The *mean score for* the two trials was subjected to multivariate analysis of variance to determine ...

Roman slaves probably had a	much lower than average life expectancy.
The Roman nobility probably had a	much higher than average life expectancy.

Describing ranges
The respondents had practised X for an average of 15 years (range 6 to 35 years).
The participants were aged 19 to 25 and were from both rural and urban backgrounds.
They calculated ranges of journal use from 10.7%–36.4% for the humanities, 25%–57% for ...
The evidence shows that life expectancy from birth lies in the range of twenty to thirty years.
The mean income of the bottom 20 percent of U.S. families declined from $10,716 to $9,833.
Rates of decline ranged from 2.71– 0.08 cm per day (Table 11) with a mean of 0.97 cm per day.
Most estimates of X range from 200.000 to 700.000 and, in some cases, up to a million or more.
At between 575 and 590 metres depth, the sea floor is extremely flat, with an average slope of ...

Describing ratios and proportions
X has the highest proportion of....
X had the lowest proportion of Y at only 14 per cent.
The annual birth rate dropped from 44.4 to 38.6 per 1000 per annum.
The proportion of live births outside marriage reached one in ten in 1945.
The proportion of the population attending university in 1990 was 65% higher than in ...

Cold weather may kill	up to about nearly almost around more than	ten times	as many people as	as hot weather.

Explaining Causality

A great deal of academic work involves understanding and suggesting solutions to problems. At postgraduate level, particularly in applied fields, students search out problems to study. In fact, one could say that problems are the raw material for a significant proportion of academic activity. However, solutions cannot be suggested unless the problem is fully analysed, and this involves a thorough understanding of the causes. Some of the language that you may find useful for explaining causes and effects is listed below.

Verbs indicating causality

Lack of iron in the diet	may cause can lead to can result in can give rise to	tiredness and fatigue.

Scurvy is a disease	caused by resulting from stemming from	lack of vitamin C.

Much of the instability in X	is driven by stems from is caused by can be attributed to	the economic effects of the war.

Nouns indicating causality

One *reason* why Xs have declined is that ...
A *consequence* of vitamin A deficiency is blindness.
X can have profound health *consequences* for older people.
The most likely *causes* of X are poor diet and lack of exercise.
The *causes* of X have been the subject of intense debate within ...

Prepositional phrases indicating causality

Around 200,000 people per year suffer from X	owing to because of as a result of as a consequence of	poor diet.

Sentence connectors indicating causality

If undernourished children do survive to become adults, they have decreased learning ability.	Therefore, Consequently, Because of this, As a result (of this),	when they grow up, it will probably be difficult for them to find work.

Adverbial elements indicating causality

Malnutrition leads to illness and a reduced ability to work in adulthood,	thus	perpetuating the poverty cycle.
The warm air rises above the surface of the sea,	thereby	creating an area of low pressure.

Nouns indicating contributing agency

X is a key *factor* in ...
X is a major *influence* on ...
X has a positive *effect* on ...
X has a significant *impact* on ...
X is an important *determinant* of ...
X and Y are important driving *factors* of Z.
X is generally seen as a *factor* strongly related to Y.
X is a significant contributory *factor* to the development of ...
This work has revealed several *factors* that are responsible for ...
The study found that loneliness has twice the *impact* on early death as obesity does.

X is a(n)	risk critical common dominant predictive important significant underlying contributing confounding complicating	factor	in ... for ...

Verbs indicating contributing agency

X *has contributed to* the decline in ...
It is now understood that X *plays* an important *role* in ...
A number of factors *play a role* in determining the effects of ...
The mixing of X and Y *exerts* a powerful *effect* upon Z through...
Recent research has revealed that X *has* a detrimental *effect* on ...
A number of factors are known *to affect* the volume and type of ...
All these factors can *impact on* the efficiency and effectiveness of ...
X is only one of many factors that help to *determine* the quality of ...

Several factors are known to	affect X. shape X. predict X. increase X. influence X. determine X. encourage X. affect the rate of ... be associated with ... increase the risk of ... play a role in determining X. be partially responsible for ...

Contributory agency		
X	aids fuels assists boosts fosters enables amplifies facilitates promotes intensifies speeds up stimulates aggravates accelerates encourages exacerbates	Y

Preventative agency		
X	blocks deters delays shrinks impairs inhibits hinders reduces controls weakens impedes prevents obstructs decreases moderates counteracts	Y

Indicating a possible causal relationship
X may be an important factor in ...
X may contribute to the increase in ...
X may play a vital role in bringing about ...
X may have been caused by an increase in ...
There is some evidence that X may affect Y.
These findings suggest that X could improve ...
It is not yet clear whether X is made worse by Y.

Indicating a possible association
X appears to be linked to Y.
The use of X may be linked to ...
In many cases, X may be associated with ...
In the literature, X has been associated with Y.
A high consumption of X could be associated with ...
This suggests a weak link may exist between X and Y.

Speculating on causes in the past

X may have	caused Y. given rise to Y. brought about Y. been an important factor in Y. contributed to the increase in Y. been caused by an increase in Y. played a vital role in bringing about Y.

X may have been	due to Y. caused by Y. attributed to Y. brought about by Y.

Verbs describing activity to understand causes

Few studies Many studies Previous studies	have	analysed explored described examined addressed investigated	the causes of X.

Giving Examples as Support

Writers may give specific examples as evidence to support their general claims or arguments. Examples can also be used to help the reader or listener understand unfamiliar or difficult concepts, and they tend to be easier to remember. For this reason, they are often used in teaching. Finally, students may be required to give examples in their work to demonstrate that they have understood a complex problem or concept. When statements and arguments are supported with examples, it is helpful to the reader when explicit language is used to signal this.

Giving examples as the main information in a sentence

A classic A useful A notable A prominent An important A well-known	example of X is ....

For example, the word 'doctor' used to mean a 'learned man'.
For example, Smith (2015) conducted a series of semi-structured interviews in ...
People begin smoking for a variety of reasons. They may, for example, be influenced by ....

Another example of what is meant by X is ...
This is exemplified in the work undertaken by ...
To give a well-known example for the sake of clarity, ...
This distinction is further exemplified in studies using ...
An example of this is the study carried out by Smith (2004) in which ...
The effectiveness of the X technique has been exemplified in a report by Smith *et al.* (2015).

This is evident in the case of ...
This is certainly true in the case of ...
The case of X illustrates the nature of ...
The evidence of X can be clearly seen in the case of ...
In a similar case in America, Smith (2015) identified ...
This can be seen in the case of the two London physics laboratories which ...

X is a good illustration of ...
X illustrates this point clearly.
This can be illustrated briefly by ...
The most dramatic illustration of this is ...
By way of illustration, Smith (2020) shows how the data for ...
These experiments illustrate that X and Y have distinct functions in ...

Giving examples as additional information in a sentence
People begin smoking for a variety of reasons, *such as* pressure from peers or ...
The prices of resources, *such as* copper, iron ore, and aluminium, have declined over ...
Many diseases can result at least in part from stress*, including*: arthritis, asthma, and migraine.
Gassendi kept in close contact with many other scholars, *such as* Kepler, Galileo, Descartes, and ...
Pavlov found that if some other stimulus, *for example* the ringing of a bell, preceded the food, the ...

Reporting cases as support
This case has shown that ...
This has been seen in the case of ...
The case reported here illustrates the ...
From these examples, it is evident that ...
Overall, these cases support the view that ...
This case study confirms the importance of ...
It is evident from the examples given here that ...
The evidence presented thus far supports the idea that ...
This case demonstrates the need for better strategies for ...
As this case very clearly demonstrates, it is important that ...
This case reveals the need for further investigation in patients with ...
This case demonstrates how X used innovative marketing strategies in ...
Recent cases reported by Smith *et al.* (2022) also support the hypothesis that ...
In support of this approach, Y has been shown to induce Z in several cases (Smith *et al.*, 2015).

This case These cases	illustrate(s) demonstrate(s)	the need for ... the dangers of ... the necessity of ... the possibility of ... the benefit of using ... how important it is to ... what can happen when ... the potential harm from ... the central role played by ... (some of) the problems caused by ... (some of) the differences between ... (some of) the difficulties that arise when ...

Indicating Shared Knowledge or Understanding

Sometimes a writer wishes to show that they are aware that an observation is probably shared by the reader or that a fact is known by other members of the academic discipline. Phrases for signalling this are listed below.

Assuming shared understanding with the reader
Of course, ...
Quite clearly, ...
It is clear that ...
It is obvious that ...
It is undeniable that ...
There is now no doubt that ...
Given this situation, it is hardly surprising that ...
One should not, of course, accept without question all ...

It is, of course,	true that ... difficult to ... possible that ... inevitable that ... recognised that ... often the case that ... debatable whether ... unrealistic to expect ... entirely possible that ... too early to say whether ... important to acknowledge ... legitimate and highly desirable for ... important to be very cautious about ... impossible to arrive at a very reliable estimate of ...

Smith	is was	clearly obviously	right correct	to	include ... criticise ... say that ... highlight ... question ... argue that ... point out that ... draw our attention to ... stress the importance of ...

Indicating shared knowledge within a discipline

As is well known,
As has been shown ...
It is well known that ...
It is a well-known fact that ...
There is now broad consensus that ...
Smith's well-known argument is that ...
It is well known among social scientists that ...
What has been established and is now generally accepted is that ...
There is now a relatively large consensus across the various disciplines that ...

It is	well established that ... widely accepted that ... generally understood that ... widely acknowledged that ... common knowledge that X is ... well known from previous studies that ...

Signalling Transition

Previewing what is to follow in a paper or dissertation is like showing a map to a driver; it enables them to see where they are going. So it is useful to think of a preview section as a 'road map' for the reader. It must be accurate, but it must be easy to follow.

Writers are also expected to indicate to the reader when they are moving from one topic to another, or from one section of text to another. These are known as transition statements and examples of these, together with some previewing statements, are given below (also refer to *A note on Academic Presentations)*.

Previewing a section of text

The following is a brief description of ...
In the section that follows, it will be argued that ...
The problem of X is discussed in the following section.
A more detailed account of X is given in the following section.
The structure and functions of X will be explained in the following section.
The following part of this paper moves on to describe in greater detail the ...
This introductory section provides a brief overview of ... It then goes on to ...

In the following	pages, section, paragraphs,	I	review ... argue that ... will describe how ... will briefly discuss ... will attempt to explore ... will present two influential theories of ...
In the section	below, that follows,		

The section below The following section	reviews ... presents ... discusses ... describes ... examines ... draws together ...

What follows is	a review of ... a summary of ... an account of ... a description of ... a brief outline of ... a brief overview of ...

Previewing a short paper (also refer to *Introducing Work*)

In this paper, I argue that ...
The aim of this paper is to ...
The central thesis of this paper is that ...
This paper has been divided into four parts. This first ...

This paper	aims to ... begins by ... argues that ... gives an account of ... discusses the case of ... has been divided into ... analyses the impact of ... attempts to show that ... contests the claim that ... provides an overview of ... first gives a brief overview of ...

Previewing a chapter or section

The aim of the chapter is to introduce ...
This section will attempt to assess whether ...
This chapter is subdivided into three sections.
The central section of this paper seeks to provide a ...
Experiments described in this chapter examine the effect of ...
In this chapter, I describe the data collection procedures and ...
The second part highlights the key theoretical concepts which ...
This chapter of the dissertation is divided into two parts. The first ...
This part of the thesis discusses the findings which emerged from ...
The purpose of this chapter is to review the literature on X. It begins by ...
This chapter is divided into four main sections, each of which presents the results relating to ...
This chapter discusses the specific methods by which the research and analyses were conducted.

The main	topics issues themes periods developments	covered in this chapter are ...

This chapter	reviews ... assesses ... discusses ... draws together ... attempts to provide ... describes the methods used in this investigation. The first section ... contextualises the research by providing background information on ...

Introducing a new topic or aspect of a topic
Regarding X, ...
As regards X, ...
In terms of X, ...
In the case of X, ...
With regard to X, ...
With respect to X, ...
On the question of X, ...
As far as X is concerned, ...
Another important aspect of X is ...

Reintroducing a topic
As discussed above, ...
As explained earlier, ...
As previously stated, ...
As indicated previously, ...
As has already been noted, ...
As described on the previous page, ...
As was mentioned in the previous chapter, ...
Returning (briefly) to the (subject/issue) of X, ...
As explained in the introduction, it is clear that ...
As was pointed out in the introduction to this paper, ...

Moving from one section to the next
Turning now to ...
Let us now turn to ...
Let us now consider ...
Moving on now to consider ...
It would be useful at this stage to consider ...
Turning now to the experimental evidence on ...
Before proceeding to examine X, it is important to ...
Before explaining these theories, it is necessary to ...
Having defined what is meant by X, I will now move on to discuss ...
So far this paper has focused on X. The following section will discuss ...
Having analysed X in some detail, we are now in a position to return to ...
This chapter has demonstrated that ... It is now necessary to explain the course of ...
Having discussed how to construct X, the final section of this paper addresses ways of ...
This section has analysed the causes of X and has argued that ... The next part of this paper will ...

Moving from one section to the next whilst indicating addition, contrast or opposition
Another significant aspect of X is ...
In addition, it is important to ask ...
Unlike Smith, Jones (2014) has argued ...
In contrast to Smith, Jones (2014) maintains ...
Despite this, little progress has been made in the ...
However, this system also has a number of serious drawbacks.
On the other hand, in spite of these recent findings about the role of ...,

Summarising a section or chapter

Thus far, it has been argued that ...
The previous section has shown that ...
To conclude this section, the literature identifies ...
This section has reviewed the three key aspects of ...
In summary, it has been shown from this review that ...
This chapter has described the methods used in this investigation and it has ...
This section has attempted to provide a brief summary of the literature relating to ...
This chapter began by describing X and arguing that ... It went on to suggest that the ...
In this section, it has been explained that ... The chapter that follows moves on to consider the ...

Previewing a following chapter

The next chapter describes synthesis and evaluation of ...
A summary of the main findings, together with ..., is provided in the next chapter.
The next chapter describes the procedures and methods used in this investigation ...
In the next section, I will present the principal findings of the current investigation ...
These analytical procedures and the results obtained from them are described in the next chapter.

In the chapter that follows	I	(briefly)	review ... present ... describe ... examine ... argue that ... comment on ... use the results obtained to discuss ...

The next chapter The chapter that follows	moves on to consider ... provides an account of ... presents a case study of ... establishes the framework for ... reviews the literature related to ... explores the relationship between ... summarises the main themes that emerged ...

Writing about the Past

Writing about the past in English involves choosing from the rather complex tense system. The phrases grouped below give an indication of the uses of the main tenses in academic writing. For a comprehensive explanation of the uses of the various tenses you will need to consult an English grammar book. A good recommendation is *Practical English Usage* by Michael Swan, Oxford University Press.

Time phrases associated with the simple past tense: specific times or periods of time in the past

In 1933, Three years later, From 1933 to 1945, In the 1930s and 1940s, During the Nazi period, Between 1933 and 1945,	restrictions were placed on German academics.

For centuries, Throughout the 19th century, At the start of the 19th century, In the latter half of the 19th century, At the beginning of the 19th century, Towards the end of the 19th century, In the early years of the 19th century, At the end of the nineteenth century, In the second half of the 19th century,	authorities in X placed restrictions on academics.

In the 1930s, Half a century later, Following World War I,	Fleming actively searched for anti-bacterial agents. he was named one of the *100 Most Important People* of the century.

Describing research history with past tense constructions

The link between X and Y was established in 2000 by Smith *et al.*
The association between X and Y was not demonstrated until 2012.
Prior to the work of Smith (1983), the role of X was largely unknown.
Before 1950, the X had received only cursory attention from historians.
The construct of X was first articulated by Smith (1977) and popularised in his book: ...
It was not until the late 1960s that historians considered X worthy of scholarly attention.
Awareness of X is not recent, having possibly first been described in the 5th century BCE by ...
The next research period involved innovative laboratory work in the late 1960s and into the 1970s.

Time phrases associated with the use of the present perfect tense: past and present connected
To date, little evidence has been found associating X with Y.
Up to now, the research has tended to focus on X rather than on Y.
It is only *since* the work of Smith (2001) that the study of X has gained momentum.
So far, three factors have been identified as being potentially important: X, Y, and Z.
Since 1965, these four economies have doubled their share of world production and trade.

Until recently, there has been little interest in X.
Only in the past ten years have studies of X directly addressed how ...
Recently, these questions have been addressed by researchers in many fields.
In recent years, researchers have investigated a variety of approaches to X but ...
More recently, literature has emerged that offers contradictory findings about ...

Over the past century there has been a dramatic increase in ...
The past decade has seen the rapid development of X in many ...
Over the past 30 years there has been a significant increase in ...
Over the past two decades, major advances in molecular biology have allowed ...
Over the past few decades, the world has seen the stunning transformation of X, Y and Z.

The present perfect tense is typically used to describe recent research with several contributors
Previous studies of X have not dealt with ...
Several recent studies have revealed that ...
It has been shown that ... (Smith, 2002, Jones, 2007).
X has been intensively investigated recently due to its ...
A considerable amount of literature has been published on X.
X has been identified as a major contributing factor for the decline of ....
Factors thought to be influencing X have been explored in several studies.
The new material has been shown to enhance X (Smith, 2002, Jones, 2007).
The relationship between X and Y has been widely investigated (Smith, 2002, Jones, ...
There have been several investigations into the causes of X (Smith, 2005; Jones, 2007).

For reference to single investigations in the past, the simple past tense is normally used
X was first identified in 1992 by ...
The first detection of X came in 1992 when ...
The first systematic study of X was reported by Smith *et al.* in 1992.
The first experimental treatment of X, by Smith *et al.* [12], used a ...
An experimental demonstration of this effect was first carried out by ...
Smith and Jones (1994) were the first to describe X, and reported that ...
X was originally isolated from Y in a soil sample from ... (Smith *et al.*, 1992).

Thirty years later, Smith (1974) reported three cases of ....
In the 1950s, Smith pointed to some of the ways in which ...

In 1960,	Smith *et al.*	performed the first ... published a paper in which they described ... introduced a system of classification based on ... demonstrated that X induced in vitro resistance to ...

Writing Abstracts

An abstract is a short statement that describes a much longer piece of writing or a prospective conference presentation. Abstracts for research papers or theses should provide the reader with a quick overview of the entire study. Abstracts written for PhDs typically contain the following elements:

- Importance of the topic
  and/or
  Reference to the current literature
  and/or
  Identification of a knowledge gap
- **Aim(s) of the current study**
- Indication of the methods used
- **Statement of the key finding(s)**
- Implications of the findings
  and/or
  Value of the current study

The first three elements listed above are grouped together because, although they may substitute each other, it is possible to find all three together. However, it is also possible to find PhD abstracts where none of them are present. Of all the elements listed above, only the 'aims of the current study' and the 'statement of key findings' appear to be obligatory and so these appear here in bold. Note that all of the elements above, except 'Implications of the findings', may also be found in the introductory section of a research paper. Phrases associated with all these elements are listed below.

Highlighting the importance of the topic
X is vital for ...
X is widespread in ...
X is fundamental to ...
X plays a key role in ...
X is a classic problem in ...
X is the primary means of ...
X is a major contributor to ...
X is an important aspect of ...
X is frequently prescribed for ...
The importance of X is indisputable.
X is one of the key components of Y.
X is attracting considerable critical attention.

Reference to current literature
Several studies have documented ...
Studies of X show the importance of ...
Several attempts have been made to ...
A growing body of evidence suggests ...
X is becoming a common trend in Y research.
Recent studies related to X have shown that ...
X has been the focus of much investigation in the search for ...
X has emerged as a powerful tool in studying the behaviour of ...
There has been substantial research undertaken on the role of ...
Previous research has indicated potential associations between ...
X has attracted considerable attention, both scholarly and popular.

Identification of a knowledge gap
However, X has yet to be understood.
Previous studies of X have not dealt with ...
Researchers have not treated X in much detail.
The historiography of X largely ignores the role of Y.
Most studies in the field of X have only focused on ...
The contribution of X has received little attention within ...
For the past three decades, studies of X have been restricted to ...
The mechanisms underlying those defects are still poorly understood.
No known empirical research has focused on exploring relationships between ...
This research has been impeded by the lack of appropriate attachment measures.

Aim of the current study
The aim of this study was to ...
This study set out to examine ...
This study set out to determine whether ...
The principal objective of this project was to investigate ...
In this study, techniques for X were developed and applied to ...
The present study aimed to explore the relationship between ...

This thesis	argues ... reports on ... investigates ... analyses the roles played by ... explores the degree to which ... addresses a neglected aspect of ... aims to portray the different ways in which ... examines the chronology and geography of ... seeks to understand and explain the role of ...

Indication of methods used
The research is based on four case studies.
Contemporary source material was used to examine ...
This study provides a novel approach to quantifying X using ...
This study used a phenomenographic approach to identify the ...
An online survey provided quantitative data from 670 participants.
Questionnaire assessments of X were collected from 116 adults who ...
The study utilised a comparison control group design with three groups of ...
The research consisted of an extensive ethnographic enquiry that included ...
A combined qualitative and quantitative methodological approach was used to ...
A cross-sectional study was undertaken to explore the potential relationship between ...

Statement of key findings
Results showed that ...
This study identified ...
The findings show that ...
Respondents reported ...
The thesis concludes that ...
Analysis of X revealed that ...
The experimental data suggested that ...
Evidence is presented which shows that ...
The research presented here confirms that ...
The study identified limited evidence of the ...
The principal findings of this research are that ...
In this study, X was shown to vary in response to ...
This review found evidence that early interventions are effective in ...
The findings indicated that there was a positive relationship between ...
Significant associations for X were identified for ten variables, including ...

Implications and/or the value of the current study
The study implies that ...
The involvement of X implies that ...
It is evidently clear from the findings that ...
An implication of this is the possibility that ...
The results of this study support the view that ...
These findings provide a solid evidence base for ...
The present results highlight the detrimental effects that X has on ...

These data support further clinical development of ...
The findings can contribute to a better understanding of ...
This research provides a timely and necessary study of the ...
The findings presented in this thesis add to our understanding of ...
The research results represent a further step towards developing ...
This study should, therefore, be of value to practitioners wishing to ...
As a result of these investigations, suggestions are identified for future research.

Writing Acknowledgements

The 'acknowledgments' sections in PhD theses are not simply a polite formality. They are important because they reveal and pay tribute to the other people and to the bodies who made the research possible. Typically included are: funding organisations, research institutes, institutions, supervisors, collaborators, close colleagues and family members. In the majority of cases, the structure moves from acknowledging the more formal support (funding bodies, institutions, supervisors) to the most familiar (close friends and family members). The phrases listed below illustrate some of the ways that thanks and appreciation can be expressed.

Firstly, Secondly, Finally,	I wish to I want to I would like to	thank X extend my thanks to X give special thanks to X express my gratitude to X	for his constant for her continuous	advice. support. tolerance. patience. guidance. forbearance. reassurance. encouragement.

Most of all, In particular, First and foremost, Last but not least,	I would like to thank	my supervisor for … the University of X for … each of the participants in this study for …

I am	also very deeply forever equally eternally especially extremely immensely particularly	grateful to X for …

I owe a great deal to ...
I owe a debt of gratitude to ...
I want to express my gratitude to ...
I am indebted to my supervisors for their ...
I wish to thank X for the award of the funding which enabled me to undertake ...
I think it is essential that I thank my long term friend and companion, X, for his ...
I welcome this opportunity to thank the friends, family and colleagues who provided ...
I must express my sincere appreciation to X for her constant and continued support and patience.

My	special sincere warmest heartfelt	thanks	go to are due to	X	who has always encouraged me to ... who provided the help, guidance and support ... who has been an unstinting source of support ... who always made time to help and support me ... for his continued support and patience. for agreeing to participate in this study. for her guidance, encouragement and support. for her academic supervision and personal support.

A very special thank you goes out to ...
Thanks also to the University of X, for providing the data for ...
Thanks to the staff of X for their contributions to the research ...
My gratitude is also extended to the following funding bodies:
My acknowledgements would not be complete without thanking ...
Thank you to the participants who gave up their valuable time to ...
There were a multitude of individuals who helped me to arrive at this point, and ...
Most importantly, I would not have been able to afford to undertake this endeavour without ...

X has been	supportive and patient throughout the writing of this thesis. an unfailing source of encouragement, advice and reassurance. a continuing source of encouragement and optimism throughout. supportive and has provided me with invaluable teaching opportunities.

X has offered valuable advice on specific aspects of ...
X has provided valuable assistance with accessing online resources.
X's enthusiasm for my topic, was essential in helping me complete this project.
X has monitored my progress and offered advice and encouragement throughout.

Notes on Academic Writing

A Note on Academic Style

The principal characteristics of written academic style are listed below.

1. Academic writing is evidence-based
Perhaps the most important distinguishing feature of written academic style is that it is evidence-based. Writers support their arguments and claims with evidence from the body of knowledge relevant to their discipline. Furthermore, any research that is undertaken must make reference to previous work in the field. As a result, academic texts are rich in attributions to other writers and references to previous research, as seen in the examples below:

- *Previous studies have shown that ...*
- *These sources suggest that from the fifth century onwards ....*
- *According to the 1957 Annual Medical Report, the death of the 960 inhabitants of ...*
- *However, as has been shown elsewhere (e.g. Smith, 1992), the increase in ...*

For further examples, refer to the section on ***Referring to the Literature*** in this document**.**

In addition, general propositions are usually supported with real examples.

- *This can be seen in the case of ...*
- *A good example of this can be found in ...*

2. Academic writing contains many words of classical origin
Unlike everyday English, academic writing is characterised by a high frequency of words of classical origin (Greek and Latin). The main reason for this is that Latin was the *lingua academica* during the European renaissance; in other words, it was the international language of scholars. Even up until relatively recently, great works of science, such as Isaac Newton's *Philosophiæ Naturalis Principia Mathematica* (1687), were written in Latin. Where academic texts were written in English, words of classical origin were used for concepts and phenomena for which there was no equivalent in English.

Although the *lingua academica* of today is English, writers of academic English still tend to use words which are derived from Latin, and also, mainly through Latin texts, from Greek.

everyday words		academic words
a lot of	→	considerable
big	→	significant
bring together	→	synthesise
get rid of	→	eradicate
not enough	→	insufficient
story	→	anecdote
thing	→	object
trouble	→	difficulty
way (of doing)	→	method
worry	→	concern

There are also some changes to grammatical words (though these are not of classical origin):

everyday words		academic words
not much research not many studies isn't any evidence	→	little research few studies no evidence

3. Academic writing tends to be cautious
Academic writers are careful about the claims they make: they take care not to appear certain where some doubt may exist, and they are careful not to over-generalise. An example of this kind of transformation can be seen below. The second sentence is in academic style:

- *Drinking alcohol causes breast cancer.* →
- *Some studies suggest that drinking alcohol may increase the risk of breast cancer.*

For more examples of this kind of language, refer to the section on ***Being Cautious***.

4. Academic writing is normally impersonal
In the interests of objectivity, academic writers tend to remove themselves from the writing. The focus is on 'what' happened, 'how' it was done, and 'what' was found. The 'who' (the writer) is not normally given very much attention. This is one of the reasons why personal pronouns ('I' and 'we') tend not to be used. In addition, academic texts rarely address the reader directly and the pronoun normally used for this, 'you', is avoided. The second sentence is in academic style:

- *You could say that Churchill made some catastrophic decisions early in the War.* →
- *It can be said that Churchill made some catastrophic decisions early in the War.*

There are some exceptions: in certain disciplines, it may be appropriate for a writer to explain their personal interest in the research area. In some disciplines, the researcher may participate in the research as a participant-observer. In these cases, 'I' will be used. The example below, which illustrates the former situation, is taken from a dissertation in History.

> *I became interested in X after reading ...... I hope to convey some of my fascination for the subject, as well as expressing my admiration of the artistic achievements of those involved.*

In research undertaken by teams, for example in medicine and science, it is common for the research to be reported using the personal pronoun, e.g. 'we'.

5. Academic writing avoids contracted forms
Contracted forms (e.g. *it's, don't, isn't, aren't*) should not be used in academic writing. The only exception would be if you are transcribing a recorded conversation or interview.

6. Academic writing uses nominalisation
There is a tendency for academic writers to transform verbs (actions) into nouns. In the example below, the verb 'opened' becomes the noun 'opening'.

- *The Liverpool and Manchester railway opened in 1830. This brought increased prosperity to both cities.*
- *The opening of the Liverpool and Manchester railway in 1830 brought increased prosperity to both cities.*

As a result of this kind of transformation, academic writing is characterised by long noun phrase constructions, as in: 'The opening of the Liverpool and Manchester railway in 1830'. In certain cases, these nominalised forms can become very long and complex:

- *the effect of reducing aggressiveness by producing an ACTH-mediated condition of decreased androgen levels.*

Although this kind of construction is considered normal in scientific writing, unless the reader is familiar with the constructions, it does make reading difficult as there are so many pieces of information to process in the one sentence. There is an argument that too much nominalisation should be discouraged.

7. Academic writing avoids rhetorical questions
Questions to introduce significant new ideas are avoided, and are replaced with statements:

- *Is the welfare system good or not?* →
- *It is important to consider the effectiveness of the British welfare system.*

However, setting out a list of research questions in the introductory section of a research report is quite common.

8. Academic writing is precise and detailed
Last of all, one of the most noticeable features of academic writing is that it is very precise and detailed. This relates to the setting out and development of the thinking and the ideas, as well as to the language used in the writing.

A Note on Style in Academic Presentations

In contrast to written style, the communicative style of academic presentations tends to be much more personal and familiar. The majority of the phrases listed below serve as useful 'signposts' for spoken academic presentations. 'Signposts' help the listeners follow where the talk is going. Notice how the personal pronouns ('I', 'we', and 'you') are used in most of these phrases.

Introducing the presentation

<table>
<tr><td rowspan="2">In this paper,</td><td>I'd like to</td><td>report on a study which aimed to ...
explore a very important aspect of ...
examine two important problems facing ...
describe some of the more recent developments in ...</td></tr>
<tr><td colspan="2">I'll mainly focus on ...</td></tr>
</table>

This afternoon, I'd like to	discuss ... describe ... speak about ... present my findings on ... address the question of ...

The aim of my presentation is to	assess ... discuss ... explore ... examine... compare ... argue that ... critically evaluate ... offer a new model for ... address the question of ... explore the ways in which ... report on the findings of my study which ...

<table>
<tr><td rowspan="2">We know that X</td><td>is</td><td>fundamental to ...
a leading cause of ...
an important aspect of ...</td></tr>
<tr><td>has
plays</td><td>a critical role in ...
a pivotal role in ...</td></tr>
</table>

One of the most	pressing important interesting challenging	problems in this area is ...

Defining and organising the topic

There are	three main types of X in ... many different kinds of ...

In this paper, I use the term 'X' to refer to ...
In this presentation, I am using the term 'X' to refer to ...
X can best be treated under three headings. These are: ...
I've divided my presentation into three sections. The first section ...

Indicating sequence

First of all, To begin with, In the first part of this paper,	I'd like to talk about ...	and then (I'll) go on to ...

I'll begin by ...
I'll then go on to ...
Another important aspect of X is ...
Finally, I'll argue that ...
Finally, I'd like to consider X.

Highlighting statements

There are two important	causes of ... reasons for ... consequences of ...

It is worth noting that ...
It is important to stress that ...
Perhaps the most interesting aspect of this is ...
What is important for us to recognise here, is that ...

Referring to a visual

If we could	focus for a moment on Figure 1, ... turn for a moment to look at Table 2,	we can see that ...

Here we can see that ...
This can be clearly seen when we look at ...
We can see this clearly in the following diagram:

Indicating transition

I'd like now to move on to	discuss ... examine ... consider ... address the question of ...

Turning now to ...
Moving on to look at the relationship between ...,
Having looked at ..., I'd now like to move on to discuss ...
Before I move on to consider X, I'd like to briefly look at ...

Concluding a talk

In this presentation, I’ve	shown that ... argued that ... explained that ...

So, to conclude, ...
I’d like to conclude by saying that ...
In conclusion, I'd like to suggest that ...

Are there any questions?
Does anyone have any questions?
That covers the main points. If you have any questions, I'll be happy to answer them.

A Note on British and US Spelling

The most common difference which is noticed in academic writing concerns verbs which end in *ise/yse* Br. or *ize/yze* US:

- *analyse* Br. v *analyze* US.
- *industrialise* Br. v *industrialize* US.
- *summarise* Br. v *summarize* US.

This difference also affects the nouns derived from the verbs:

- *organisation* Br. v *organization* US.
- *globalisation* Br. v *globalization* US.
- *colonisation* Br. v *colonization* US.

Another noticeable difference relates to words ending in *re*:

- *centre* Br. v *center* US.
- *metre* Br. v *meter* US.
- *litre* Br. v *liter* US.

Below are some other differences. Can you see any patterns?

British	US
aeroplane	*airplane*
analogue	*analog*
behaviour	*behavior*
catalogue	*catalog*
colour	*color*
connection	*connexion*
defence	*defense*
dialogue	*dialog*
endeavour	*endeavor*
encyclopaedia	*encyclopedia*
fibre	*fiber*
foetus	*fetus*
instalment	*installment*
labour	*labor*
paediatric	*pediatric*
plough	*plow*
programme	*program*
rigour	*rigor*
sceptical	*skeptical*
skilful	*skillful*
travelled	*traveled*

If you are writing for a British university or a British journal, you should use the British spelling. If you are writing for a US university or journal, you should use the US spelling.

A Note on Using Gender-Neutral Language

Although there may be situations in academic writing where it is necessary to indicate gender, as a general rule it is preferable to use language that avoids this.

Referring to specific roles

Professional roles should be gender neutral, as in the following examples:

- chairman/chairwoman → chair or chairperson
- policeman/policewoman → police officer
- businessman/businesswoman → businessperson, business executive, person in business
- salesmen/saleswoman → sales associate, salesperson, sales executive

Referring to individuals

Where the gender of an individual is known, it is appropriate to refer to them using gendered pronouns: *he/his* or *she/her*.

- In *her* analysis of X, Smith (2020) seeks to challenge ... ✓

Where the gender of an individual is unknown or irrelevant, you should refer to them using *they/their*:

- Participant 24 commented that *they* had not experienced ... ✓

Referring to people generally

You should avoid using *he* or *she* when referring to people generally. In this case, it is preferable to change the subject to a gender-neutral word and to use a gender-neutral pronoun.

- It is important for a *man* to seek help if ... *He* should contact ... X
- It is important for a *person* to seek help if ... *They* should contact ...✓

Referring to humans

Avoid the use of *man* or *mankind* when referring to humans in general. Instead, you should use: *humans, humanity, humankind.*

A Note on Punctuation

As the purpose of punctuation is to make written English easier to read and to make the meaning clear and unambiguous, good, accurate punctuation is important in academic writing. The following notes highlight points of particular relevance to academic writing.

1. Full stop .

- To indicate the end of a sentence
- To indicate an abbreviation such as *etc., et al.* (not always used)
- To indicate an omission in a quoted text [**...**].

2. Comma ,

- To separate two main parts of a sentence (two clauses) joined by words such as *and, or, but,*
- To separate a dependent part of a sentence (beginning with words such as *although, when, because*) from the main part, particularly if the dependent part comes first in the sentence
- To indicate additional information*, however relevant it may be,* in a sentence
- To indicate a non-defining relative clause*, which simply provides additional information,* in a sentence
- To separate items in a list such as: *apples, oranges, and pears* (note that the final comma before *and* is often omitted).

3. Colon :

- To introduce an explanation: *The reason the experiment failed was obvious: the equipment was faulty.*
- To introduce a list, particularly a grammatically complex list. See the example below under *semi-colon*
- To introduce a direct quotation, particularly a long one: *Jones (2003) states that: ' '.*

4. Semi-colon ;

- To separate two sentences that are very closely connected in meaning (instead of using a full stop): *Some students prefer to write essays; others prefer to give presentations.*
- To separate clearly items in a grammatically complex list: *For Aristotle, motion* is of four kinds*: (1) motion which ...; (2) motion which ...; (3) motion which ...; and (4) motion which...*

5. Quotation marks ' ' / " "

- To indicate a direct quotation
- To highlight words or phrases used in a special or unusual way: *Quotation marks are also called 'inverted commas' or 'speech marks'.*

NB Single quotation marks now seem to be more commonly used than double. For quotations within quotations, use double quotation marks inside single (or single inside double).

6. Dash –

- Generally, it is best to avoid this in formal academic writing. Instead use a colon, semi-colon, or brackets, as appropriate.

A Note on Article Use

Article use in English is a very complex area. However, there are a few simple rules which will help you in many situations and these are explained below:

1. Singular countable nouns

All singular countable nouns are always preceded by a small modifying word known in grammar as a determiner, and this is often an article (*a/an, the*). Countable words which are common in academic writing and which often cause problems for non-native speakers of English, include: *system, model, method, approach, group, problem, effect, level, investigation, sector, study, participant, condition, category*

Note that even if these words are preceded by attributive nouns or adjectives, a determiner is still needed:

- *the greenhouse effect, the transport system, the control group*
- *a high level, a systematic approach, a rigorous study, an exploratory investigation*

2. Plural countable nouns

If the writer is thinking about a specific group, then the definite article is normally used: *The books in this collection were published in the 19th or early 20th century.*

Otherwise no article is used:

- *Learners tend to remember new facts when they are contextualised.*

3. Uncountable nouns

Uncountable nouns are not normally accompanied by an article:

- *Science has been defined as a systematic approach to answering questions.*
- *Reliability is an important quality of any test.*

But if they are post-modified by *of....,* or *which* ... the definite article is normally used:

- *The science of global warming is a complex and controversial area.*
- *The reliability of this instrument is poor.*
- *Chemistry is the science which addresses the composition and behaviour of matter.*

4. Names

Names and titles are not normally preceded by the definite article (*the*)

- *Manchester University, Manchester*

But this changes if the noun phrase contains a post-modifying structure (*of …*)

- *The University of Manchester,* *The United States of America*

or if they contain words like *organisation, association or institute*

- *The World Health Organisation, The American Heart Association, The Royal Society. The SETI Institute*

Apart from these simple rules, the other thing you need to do is to check how noun phrases are used in the texts that you read. Make a mental note of this as you read, or check back to the source text when you are writing.

A Note on Sentence Structure

1. Simple sentences

In written English, all sentences contain a Subject → Verb structure. The subject always precedes the verb, except in questions where the order is reversed.

S	V	
An electron	*is*	*an elementary particle.*

The subject may be one word, but it is usually a group of words centred around a noun. The verb, which can indicate an action, a state, or simply serve to link the subject to other information, may also consist of more than one word. Various other sentence elements may be placed before or after the Subject → Verb structure:

	S	V	
Between 1933 and 1945,	*restrictions*	*were placed*	*on German academics.*

It is common for the subject to consist of many words:

S	V	
The information on various types of wasps and bees in the report	*was*	*useful to environmentalists who were fighting the use of pesticides.*

Sometimes, however, the subject and verb can just be one word each:

S	V	
It	*is*	*almost certain that a lower speed limit will result in fewer injuries to pedestrians.*

These simple sentences always end with a full stop. In academic writing, however, many sentences are more complicated than this simple pattern.

2. Complex sentences

Many sentences contain more than one Subject → Verb structure, but in a complex sentence one of these parts (known grammatically as clauses) will convey the main meaning and will make sense by itself:

Dependent part			Main part	
S	V		S	V
Although recent research	*has shown*	*X,*	*no controlled studies*	*have been reported.*

The main part of the sentence is also known as the independent part.

The main part of the sentence can also be placed before the dependent part.

Main part

S	V	
Oral societies	*tend to be*	*more concerned with the present*

Dependent part

	S	V	
whereas	*literate societies*	*have*	*a very definite awareness of the past.*

The dependent part of complex sentence is usually preceded by a word or phrase such as: *although, even though, if, even if, when, because, as, since, whereas, while* (refer to ***subordinators*** on the next page).

3. Compound sentences

Some sentences may have two Subject → Verb structures and each of these convey meaning that can make sense by itself; in other words, there are two main parts. The two parts may be joined by words like *and, or, but, so,* or by using a semi-colon (;) .

S	V	
Supporters of the 'Great Divide' theory	*agree*	*that something is lost as well as gained when people become literate,*

	S	V	
but	*they*	*consider*	*it is worth losing some benefits in order to obtain many others.*

4. Common problems relating to sentence structure

It is incorrect to write the dependent part of a complex sentence as a complete sentence with a full stop:

- *Whereas literate societies have a very definite awareness of the past.* X
- *Although a number of studies have been undertaken.* X

It is incorrect to write two independent parts as one sentence without a joining word.

- *Supporters of the 'Great Divide' theory agree that something is lost as well as gained when people become literate, they consider it is worth losing some benefits in order to obtain many others.* X

A Note on Paragraph Structure

A pattern that can be identified in many well-written paragraphs is that of a controlling idea followed by supporting information. The controlling idea, sometimes referred to as the *topic sentence*, introduces a new idea, topic, argument or piece of information into the main text. This is then either explained further or supported by subsequent sentences. This structure can be represented schematically thus:

Topic Sentence (new point, expressed in general terms)
Supporting Information which may include a combination of: • statistics • examples • quotations • a development in time • an explanation or reason • specific aspects or details • an effect or consequence • reference to previous research

It is important that the explanatory or supporting information in a paragraph should relate to the topic sentence. If new points or ideas are to be stated, then these should be treated in a separate paragraph. It is also important that the explanatory or supporting information should not repeat the general ideas expressed in the topic sentence.

An example of the kind of paragraph structure suggested above is given below. Note the development from the general idea to the more detailed information. Also note the thematic linking, which is signalled by the words in bold, between the sentences. Each of these words and phrases links back to an idea introduced in the previous sentence. Here, the sentences have been separated and numbered.

1. Many children become interested in competitive sport at early ages. →

2. Early involvement (prior to maturity) in **competitive sport** often exposes individuals to types of stress that may affect their growth, producing a disruption of the normal growth pattern (Wang, 1988; Brown, 1998). →

3. Among cyclists the most potentially serious of **these disorders** is likely to be increased thoracic curvature. →

4. **Cycling** alters the anatomical position of the spine (to a flexed position) particularly the thoracic spine, and exposes the anterior portion of the vertebral column to higher compression (Smith, 1998; Jones, 2012).

A Note on the Writing Process

So far this document has been about 'what we write'. The following section comprises a set of notes which are concerned with 'how' we write. It is organised into a series of helpful tips. Although only two pages are devoted to these ideas, together they have the potential to make a significant deference to the quality and quantity of your written output.

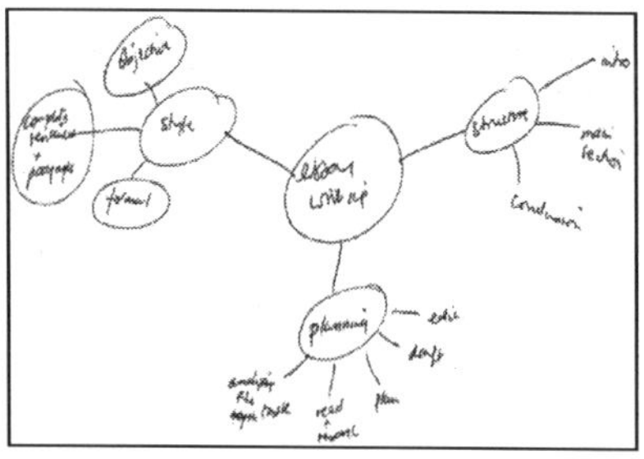

Tip No. 1. The importance of planning: Research has shown that experienced writers plan extensively. Initially, planning may involve simply generating ideas and exploring the relationships between them schematically, as in the diagram to the right. At a more advanced stage of the planning process, a chapter outline of the thesis or dissertation will be necessary. This will become more detailed as you work on your study. You need to think of a writing plan as a road map. Without a map, you will probably lose your way or travel in circles.

Tip No. 2. Getting started: Many writers suffer from 'writers' block'; they find it difficult to get started. One way of overcoming this is to give yourself a short period of time (say four minutes), and without stopping, write whatever comes into your mind about the topic. The important thing to do is to keep writing, or if you are using a keyboard, to keep typing. Don't worry about spelling of grammar – just keep producing words. You will be surprised at how much text you will produce, and how many ideas are generated in such a short time. Now you can begin to organise the ideas you have produced, ensuring that they are written in logically developed and grammatically correct sentences.

Tip No. 3. Be regular: You should timetable yourself so that you have a regular daily writing slot. This may seem obvious, but it is fundamental to ensuring the production of written text. Timetable a writing period each day, and aim to produce some text every time. How much you produce will vary, and what you produce, even if it is just a few paragraphs, may only be in the initial draft stage. This is not so important. The important thing is that the writing becomes a part of your daily routine. Simply getting your body to sit in front of a computer at a certain time each day will produce results.

Tip No. 4. Keep a notebook: When we are writing up a major piece of work, many ideas and insights come to us when we are not actually writing. Often, some of the most insightful ideas emerge when we are in a non-focused cognitive state, such as when we are walking, running, or swimming. Unless you can capture these ideas soon after they come to you, they may be lost. A small notebook and a pen is probably the best way to capture these thoughts before they disappear. The notebook itself can become a place where you develop the ideas and even start to formulate how the ideas will be developed in textual form.

Tip No. 5. Understand the recursive process: Writing at the academic level is not something we can do once and then leave. It is a recursive process. This means writers return to their initial texts, revising and redrafting them. This process is ongoing. In fact, many writers find it difficult to stop improving their writing, but with time being limited, they try to do as much as they can before the onset of a particular deadline. One thing we do know: successful writers write initial drafts, redraft, work on final drafts and then edit their work.

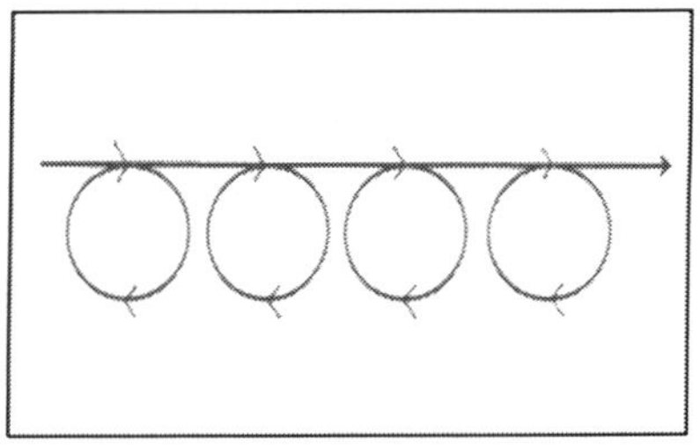

Tip No. 6. Read your own writing: Read what you have written back to yourself, out loud if necessary, and ask yourself: i) do I understand what I have written? ii) does it sound natural? Reading your text out load is actually the best way of checking this. If what you have written does not sound right to you when you do this, it is probably badly written. One famous French writer (Gustav Flaubert) used to shout out his manuscripts before sending them off to be published. He claimed that bad writing never passed this simple test.

Tip No. 7. Stand back from your writing: Think of yourself as a mountain climber. Most climbers, during a climb, can only see a few feet in front of their faces. They cannot see the whole mountain. They can see other mountains, but not the one they are climbing. To do this they need to move a few kilometres away. At such a distance, they can see the route they are planning and they can see how their planned route moves up the mountain. As a writer, you should ask yourself: Is the route to the 'top' unbroken? Do all the minor 'steps' move upwards? Can the minor 'steps' be 'carried out' more clearly? The best way to create a sense of distance with your writing is with time: Leave it a few days, or longer, and comeback to your writing with fresh eyes and with a better sense of the overall structure.

Tip No. 8. Talk about your writing: Writing is a very solitary activity and we tend not to talk about it to others. This is quite strange given that we spend so many hours on this activity. Asking another person to read some of what you have written and to give feedback can be a very useful experience; particularly if the feedback is reciprocal and both of you receive constructive criticism. It is worth bearing in mind that academic writers often receive their papers back from journal editors or publishers asking them to make changes. You might also consider forming a group of writers like yourself. Together you can read each other's writing and share the feedback.

Useful Lists

A List of Words and Phrases for Connecting Ideas

As well as using simple conjunctions (e.g., *and, but, or*) to link ideas, academic writers have available to them a broad range of more sophisticated words and phrases. Some of the more commonly used ones are listed below.

	Words and phrases which link ideas across two sentences[1]	**Words or phrases which precede a noun phrase**[2]	**Subordinators: express relationships within one sentence (with two clauses)**[3]
Addition	*also* *moreover* *in addition* *furthermore*	*in addition to*	
Adversativity	*yet* *however* *nevertheless* *on the other hand*	*despite* *in spite of*	*although* *even though*
Aspect	*in this respect* *in other respects* *from this perspective*		
Clarification	*that is* *in other words*		
Consequence	*thus* *hence* *therefore* *as a result* *consequently*		
Contrast	*however* *in contrast* *on the other hand*	*unlike* *in contrast to*	*while* *whereas*
Illustration	*for example* *for instance*		
Reason		*due to* *owing to* *because of* *on account of*	*as* *since* *because*
Sequence	*firstly* *first of all* *secondly* *finally* *in conclusion*		

[1] He did not sleep very much. *However*, he still managed to pass the exam.
He did not sleep very much; *however*, he still managed to pass the exam.

[2] *Despite* the lack of sleep, he still managed to pass the exam.
He still managed to pass the exam *despite* the lack of sleep.

[3] *Even though* he was unable to sleep, he still managed to pass the exam.
He still managed to pass the exam *even though* he was unable to sleep.

A List of Commonly Used Verbs

The tables below contain a list of verbs that can be found in academic writing. The list, which is organised alphabetically, only includes the more generic and commonly used verbs. Note that British spellings are used. Most of the verbs below are found in the *Academic Phrasebank* and a small number of additional verbs have been drawn from Coxhead's *Academic Word List*. https://www.wgtn.ac.nz/lals/resources/academicwordlist/awl-headwords

A	arise	claim	consume	devote	exacerbate
abandon	arrange	clarify	contradict	differ	examine
accelerate	ascertain	classify	contrast	differentiate	exceed
accentuate	assay	code	contribute	diminish	exclude
accept	assemble	coincide	control	discover	execute
access	assert	collapse	convene	discriminate	exemplify
accommodate	assess	collect	converse	discuss	exist
accompany	assign	commence	convert	display	experience
accomplish	assist	comment	convince	displace	experiment
account for	associate	commit	cooperate	dispute	explain
accumulate	assume	communicate	coordinate	dissect	explore
achieve	assure	compare	counteract	dispose	express
acknowledge	attach	compensate	correspond	distinguish	extend
acquire	attain	compile	corroborate	divide	extract
adapt	attempt	complement	cover	document	extrapolate
add to	attend	complete	create	draft	
adopt	attract	compose	credit	draw from	**F**
address	attribute	comprehend	criticise	draw together	fabricate
adjust	automate	comprise	critique	draw (up)on	facilitate
administer	avoid	compute		draw up	fail
advocate		concede	**D**	drive	familiarise
affect	**B**	conceive	date		find
aggravate	base on	concentrate	deal with	**E**	fluctuate
aggregate	benefit	conceptualise	debate	edit	focus
agree	boost	concern	decline	elicit	format
aid	broaden	conclude	decrease	eliminate	formulate
allocate	brief	conduct	deduce	elucidate	foster
allow	bring about	confer	defend	embody	found
alter		confine	define	embrace	
amend	**C**	confirm	delay	emerge	**G**
amplify	calculate	conflict	demonstrate	employ	gain
analyse	capture	conform	denote	enable	gather
anonymise	carry out	confound	deny	encompass	gauge
anticipate	cast doubt on	connect	depress	encourage	generalise
append	categorise	consent	derive	engage	generate
apply	cause	consider	describe	enhance	grade
appraise	caution	consist	design	ensure	grant
appreciate	cease	constitute	detect	equate	grasp
approach	challenge	constrain	deter	establish	group
approve	change	contradict	determine	estimate	grow
approximate	channel	construct	develop	evaluate	guarantee
argue	cite	consult	deviate	evolve	

H
heighten
highlight
hinder
hold
hypothesise

I
identify
ignore
illustrate
impair
impede
implement
implicate
imply
impose
improve
incline
include
incorporate
increase
include
indicate
induce
influence
inhibit
initiate
infer
influence
innovate
input
insert
insist
inspect
instruct
integrate
intensify
interact
interfere
interpret
intervene
interview
introduce
invest
investigate
invoke
involve
isolate

J
judge
justify

L
label
lack
layer lay out
lead
lecture
level off
limit
link
list
locate

M
maintain
manipulate
match
maximise
measure
mediate
mention
migrate
minimise
mislead
model
moderate
modify
monitor

N
negate
neglect
normalise
note
notify

O
observe
obstruct
obtain
occupy
occur
offer
offset
operate
oppose
order
organise
originate
outline
overlap
overlook

P
paraphrase
participate
pay attention to
perceive
perform
perpetuate
persist
persuade
pinpoint
pioneer
play a role
plot
point to/ towards
point out
popularise
pose
postulate
prepare
precede
preclude
predict
prescribe
present
presume
prevent
prioritise
proceed
prohibit
project
promote
prompt
propose
proscribe
prove
provide
publish
pursue

Q
qualify
quantify
quote
question

R
raise
rank rate
reach
react
recall
recognise
recommend
record
recover
recruit
reduce
refer
refine
reflect
refuse
regard
register
regulate
reinforce
reject
relate
relax
release
relinquish
rely
remain
remedy
remark
remind
remove
renew
repeat
report
represent
require
research
reside
resolve
respond
restate
restore
restrain
restrict
result from
result in
retain
reverse
reveal
retrieve
review
revise
rise
rule out

S
search
secure
seek
select
separate
sequence
serve
set out
set up
shed light on
shift
show
signify
simplify
simulate
skew
solve
source
speculate
specify
speed up
state
stimulate
stress
structure
struggle
subdivide
subject to
submit
subscribe
substantiate
substitute
succeed
suffer
suggest
summarise
supplement
support
surrender
survey
sustain
synthesise
survive
suspend

T
tabulate
tackle
take into account
take issue with
target
tend
terminate
test
throw up
tie together
trace
transfer
transform
transcribe
translate
transmit
treat
trigger

U
underestimate
undergo
underlie
understand
undertake
unify
use
utilise

V
validate
value
vary
violate
visualise

W
weaken
withstand
witness

A List of Commonly Confused Words

Your spellchecker will only indicate words that are misspelt which it does not recognise. However, if the word that you have misspelt is correct when it has a different meaning, the spellchecker will not show you the correct form of the word you want. In these cases, the writer has to know the correct spelling. The list below contains words which are commonly misspelt, as well as words which may be spelt correctly but which are simply confused.

abbreviation/acronym
An *abbreviation* is a shortened form of a word or phrase. Usually, but not always, it consists of a letter or group of letters taken from the word or phrase. *Dr.* and *Prof.* are common examples. An *acronym* is an abbreviation formed from the initial components in a phrase or a word. These elements in turn form a new word: *NATO, Benelux, UNESCO.*

affect/effect
Affect is a verb, e.g. *A affects B*;
Effect is a noun and is therefore, in its singular form, always used after an article/determiner ('an' or 'the'/'this'), e.g. *The Greenhouse Effect*.

compliment/complement
Compliment (verb) means to praise someone. *Complement* (verb) means to complete or add something in a way that usually improves it. Both words can also be used as nouns.

comprise/consist
Both words mean 'to be made up of', but only *consist* is accompanied by *of.*

discrete/discreet
Discrete is an adjective which means 'separate' or 'distinct'. *Discreet* is an adjective which means 'to keep silent or tactful about something'.

formerly/formally
Formerly means 'earlier'. *Formally* means 'conventionally' or 'officially'.

i.e./e.g.
i.e. is the abbreviation for *id est* which mean 'that is' or 'in other words'.
e.g. is the abbreviation for *exempli gratia* which has the same meaning as 'for example' and 'for instance'.

its/it's
its – without an apostrophe - is a possessive determiner similar to 'my' or 'your' .
it's is a contracted form of 'it is' or 'it has' . Note, however, that contracted forms are avoided in academic writing.

later/latter
Later is an adverb which means 'at an advanced point of time'. *Latter* is an adjective used to refer to an item listed in a text. It means 'most recently mentioned'; in other words, the last item.

practice/practise
In British English, *practice* is a noun and *practise* is a verb. American English allows both spellings for both forms.

precede/proceed
The verb *precede* means 'to come before'. The verb *proceed* means 'to go forward' or 'to begin to carry out'.

principle/principal
Principle is a noun which means 'a basic belief, theory or rule'. *Principal* is an adjective which means 'main' or 'most important'; it can also refer to a head teacher of a school or college, in which case it is a noun.

there/their
There is used to indicate the existence of something, e.g. *There are two famous football teams in Manchester.* The word *their* is used to indicate possession, i.e. if something belongs to someone or something.

prescribe/proscribe
The verb *prescribe* means to advise or authorise the use of something. The verb *proscribe* means to forbid or to restrict.

The Word *Evidence* and some of its Common Collocations

The word *evidence* can be found in many sections of *Academic Phrasebank,* particularly in those sections which relate the main parts of a research paper, dissertation or thesis. In academic writing, the word has a precise meaning: it refers to information that has been systematically collected and analysed using well-described and approved methods, and which - following analysis and discussion - is then shared with other researchers through publication. Academic writers critically examine the research evidence of others in their field. They then build on this by contributing their own research evidence (findings) to that existing body of knowledge. Words which are often used in conjunction with the word *evidence,* i.e. its collocations, are listed below.

Adjectives denoting type of *evidence*

clinical archival indirect historical empirical statistical anecdotal supporting documentary experimental archeological observational epidemiological	evidence

Commonly used adjectives and adverbs denoting strength of *evidence*

The	current existing available	evidence for X is	very quite rather particularly	weak. flimsy. limited. inconsistent. unconvincing. controversial.
				clear. strong. convincing. persuasive. compelling. encouraging.

Commonly used premodifying adjectives denoting strength of *evidence*

There is	no* little scant limited insufficient some* growing mounting emerging increasing accumulating good strong robust ample reliable sufficient convincing widespread considerable	evidence that ... evidence to suggest that ...

**no* and *some* are not adjectives

Commonly used adverbs and verbs with *evidence*

The evidence presented	here above thus far up to now in this paper in this thesis in this review	shows that ... suggests that ... confirms that ... casts doubt on ... clearly indicates ... points to a need for ... supports the view that ... provides some support for ... raises important questions about ... highlights the important role that ... has three important policy implications. challenges our current understanding of ... indicates a need to monitor and improve ...

Printed in Great Britain
by Amazon

26500337R00099